The Nature of True Prayer

By F. L. RAWSON

Member of the Institution of Electrical Engineers and Associate
Member of the Institution of Civil Engineers

Sixth Edition, 1930

LONDON, ENGLAND
THE SOCIETY FOR SPREADING
THE KNOWLEDGE OF
TRUE PRAYER

PUBLISHER'S NOTE

THE author of **The Nature of True Prayer,** who devoted his life to the healing, teaching and preaching work of Right Thinking True Prayer, founded The Society for Spreading the Knowledge of True Prayer and its weekly magazine *Active Service,* with the object of establishing an impersonal means of carrying forward the work. This the Society is doing by means of its publications and other modes of carrying on the healing and teaching activities involved in the necessity for the practice of the standpoint.

Active Service continues to operate as the Society's official organ.

London, England. *The S.S.K.T.P.*

PRINTED IN GREAT BRITAIN BY
MORRISON AND GIBB LTD., LONDON AND EDINBURGH

CHAPTER I

THE NATURE OF TRUE PRAYER

THE Walker Trustees some time ago offered a prize of £100 for what they described as " the most widely helpful essay—open to anyone in any part of the world who may choose to compete—on the subject of prayer : the meaning, the reality, and the power of prayer : its place and value to the individual, to the Church, and to the State ; in the everyday affairs of life, in the healing of sickness and disease ; in times of 10 distress and of national danger, and in relation to national ideals and to world progress."

They also truly said : " At this time of world tragedy the significance of prayer in daily life is everywhere becoming more widely recognized, and it is felt that the time may have come for gathering together a record of the thoughts of those who have realized its meaning and power and are willing to share their experiences with others." *

As the main object of *Active Service* † is to help humanity to gain a knowledge of true prayer as taught and 20 demonstrated by Jesus the Christ, it seems fitting to commence this series of articles on " How to obtain a better understanding of Truth," by one on the subject of prayer.

The Evolution of Prayer.

It is evident that the basis of true prayer must be Scientific Right Thinking, as prayer is entirely a matter of what one thinks or realizes. Prayer may range from desire—for, as James Montgomery writes :

> " Prayer is the soul's sincere desire,
> Uttered or unexpressed ;
> The motion of a hidden fire
> That trembles in the breast."—

30

---

* Mr. Rawson had not time to send in an essay, but in the collection of the best essays received, which was published under the title of *The Power of Prayer* (Macmillan), has been included an essay of his entitled " The Claim of Right Thinking."

† *Active Service*, a weekly paper devoted to the spreading of the knowledge of Truth. Published every Saturday, and obtainable from

The Society for Spreading the Knowledge of True Prayer

14a, Eccleston Street, London, S.W.1, England.

up to the highest form of prayer, which includes desire, and is the realization of man's highest concept of God.

In olden days prayer was sometimes mere adoration of, or prostration before, constellations, fire, animals, relics, pictures, etc. ; sometimes it was the asking of something as a favour or as a right ; sometimes a definite action, often involving gifts ; sometimes merely a sacrifice of time or position, and even of animals and human beings, with the object of currying favour with 10 some inexorable god or gods.

As time went on, the knowledge of the true nature of prayer evolved, and not only every now and then did certain men appear to gain a demonstrable knowledge of God, but this knowledge gradually spread.

From time to time, men who were pre-eminent stood out above the crowd, but their teachings did not seem to keep their hold upon the mass of humanity. Men were too material.

At the time of the Advent of our Lord, as far as can 20 be told, the whole of the world was on a purely material basis. He set his seal of authority on prayer as being conscious communion with one great God, infinite Mind.

The Master taught the true nature and character of prayer and demonstrated his teaching by giving over-whelming proofs of its truth.

At the time of his final demonstration, when his last tribute to matter was paid with his cry, " *My God, my God, why hast thou forsaken me ?* " (Mark 15 : 34) it seemed as if his teachings had ended, and he would fail 30 to justify his title of Messiah or Saviour of the world. Rising to sublime heights he again realized his unity with God and sealed his conquest over material beliefs with the words, " *It is finished.*" His work was done, and he recognized that Truth had again proved that " Love *never* faileth."

Then came his glorious victory over death, and he had to make up his mind whether he would dematerialize and retire from the war he had waged without one soul to help him, or whether he would remain and complete 40 his work for those who were still struggling along the pathway he had pointed out.

In the *Book of the Golden Precepts*, which was written thousands of years ago, speaking of the man who has gained a sufficient knowledge of Truth, it is said :—

" He shall surely reach his great reward. Shall he not use the gifts
which it confers for his own rest and bliss, his well-earned weal and
glory—he, the subduer of the great Delusion ? Compassion speaks and
saith, 'Can there be bliss when all that lives must suffer ? Shalt thou
be saved and hear the whole world cry ?' . . . if thou wouldst be
Tathagata, follow upon thy predecessor's steps, remain unselfish till the
endless end. Thou art enlightened—choose the way."

Jesus chose the highest ; and it was during the forty
days in which he remained, that he raised some of his 10
disciples from a material basis on to a spiritual basis,
and the teachings that he had given them consequently
spread throughout the then known world.

Disappearance of Spirituality.

The key to the miracles of Jesus our Lord was lost
sight of and again discovered, when it was recognized
that man is not a material being liable to sin, disease, and
suffering, but a perfect being, in a perfect world, governed
by a perfect God, " *in Christ*," " *hid with Christ in
God* " (Col. 3 : 3).   20

Heaven is no future state to reach by death. We
make our own comparative heaven and our own hell by
the way we think. We may have a great deal of heaven
here and now, if we will only think heavenly thoughts.

The true method of prayer, and its resultant so-called
miracles, was lost before the fourth century, when Christianity, approved by temporal authority, became a State
belief and spirituality disappeared, submerged in forms
and ceremonies. Christianity then became a mere name,
and we had a repetition of what was described in 30
2 Chronicles 36 : 16, when the priests and people " *mocked
the messengers of God, and despised his words, and mis-
used his prophets, until the wrath of the Lord arose
against his people, till there was no healing.*" The
Hebrew word " healing " is translated " remedy " in
the authorized version, and it was the habitual instantaneous healing of sin and disease, and the elimination
of the innumerable troubles and limitations that mankind
is heir to, which was lost when the teachings of our
Lord were twisted out of all recognition and shorn of 40
their divine power.

Jerome, in his translation of the Bible, instead of the
word translated " miracle," used a word meaning " an

act of power or sign," but when, later, the Christians
were twitted with their failure to prove the truth of
their religion by their "acts of power or signs," in the
way that the founders of their faith had done, the word
was changed to the Latin word "miraculum," meaning
something against law. But God is the Principle of all
law and order, and Jesus could not possibly have performed miracles in contradiction to law. As a matter
of fact, his miracles were not supernatural, but divinely
10 natural, due to the inevitable action of a universal,
spiritual law, and performed through a knowledge of
Scientific Right Thinking.

It is only during the last fifty years that we have
begun to understand the Principle upon which the
miracles of Jesus the Christ are based.

Think Good, Good Follows ; Think Evil, Evil Follows.

There are to-day some fifty or sixty sects and probably
over a hundred schools of psychology : some millions of
mental workers in all, with many varying beliefs. They
20 all recognize the importance of thinking rightly ; there
is only one point, however, upon which they all agree,
namely, that if a man thinks good, it is followed by good ;
if he thinks evil, it is followed by evil. In other words,
we make our own comparative heaven and our own hell
by the way we think. Heaven is a perfect state of consciousness. The only power that evil has is the power
we give it in our own so-called mind by recognizing it,
thinking it real. If you stop thinking of the evil, that
is the end of the evil. It is easy to stop thinking evil
30 with the conscious mind ; for instance, read an interesting book. The difficulty is in stopping the subconscious
mind from thinking evil, and the only way in which
this can be done is by actively, consciously thinking of
good. When you think of good, however, you must
not think lies and think that you are well when you are
ill. You must not even think of the so-called good of
the material world and think strongly of what you hope
for. You have to think of absolute good, God and
heaven. In other words, you must think of an absolutely
40 perfect, ideal, mental, spiritual world in which you have
always existed, you exist now, and always will exist.
Good is always absolute, as our Lord pointed out when

he said : " *Why callest thou me good ? there is none good but one, that is God*" (Matt. 19 : 17). Evil is relative. Everything in the so-called material world is more or less evil, some so little evil that we call it good. This is because the material world is the world of reality, heaven, partly hidden by an hypothetical or imaginary " *mist* " of matter (Gen. 2 : 6), or " *vail that is spread over all nations* " (Isa. 25 : 7). This " *mist* " or " *vail* " is steadily thinning and disappearing, slowly always, rapidly when we are thinking of God and heaven. All the so-called good which we see around us is part of heaven hidden more or less by this " *mist* " of matter, which is only imaginary, but which seems to hide heaven from us. Directly we start to think of good, of God and heaven, it commences to thin and disappear. All the evil was there at the so-called commencement of the material world, which, as Kant showed, is best described as a series of cinema or moving pictures, made up of heaven and the " mist." The evil therein gradually disappears, as the mist thins, until there is nothing but the good left.

There is no intrinsic merit in thinking of the good. It is not this that brings about the desired result. When the vane points to the North, it is a sign that the North wind is blowing. It does not cause the North wind to blow. When thinking of God and heaven one stops thinking of the evil, and this is the proof that the mist is thinning and the so-called evil, which is a suppositional absence of good, is disappearing. There is no cause but God. You cannot think of what is called good and evil at the same time. Consequently it does not matter so very much what your concept of God and heaven is, so long as it is your best concept. The higher the concept, the better the result. The more the " *mist* " has thinned, the better heaven is seen. What you want to do is to get right away from all thoughts of the material world, and realize, or make as real as possible to yourself, the world of reality, heaven. When you are doing this the evil is disappearing rapidly ; otherwise it disappears very, very slowly.

If, in order to get rid of trouble, you have to think of God, then it is necessary to know something of what God is. If we try to discover from the Bible what God is, we find ourselves in difficulties, because the Bible contains the evolution of man's knowledge of God. It commences with the idea of a God Who is *remorseful* (Gen. 6 : 6), *tyrannical* (Gen. 3 : 15), *changeable* (Gen. 6 : 7), *jealous* (Ex. 20 : 5), and ends with God Who is " all in all," God Who is " *Alpha and Omega, the beginning and the end, the first and the last* " (Rev. 22 : 13).

Man is Spiritual.

There are many passages in the Bible which show that man is not material, but spiritual; for instance, in the words of the Psalmist, " *What is man, that thou art mindful of him ? . . . thou hast made him a little lower than Elohim, and hast crowned him with glory and honour. Thou madest him to have dominion* " (Ps. 8 : 4–6 ; Rev. Ver.). In other words we are, each of us, " *partakers of the divine nature* " (2 Peter 1 : 4), having dominion by prayer over every form of evil. " *Now are we the sons of God* " (1 John 3 : 2), " *in Christ* " (Rom. 12 : 5), " *hid with Christ in God* " (Col. 3 : 3). The Christ is the highest possible thing next to God without being God, namely, the true idea of God and His manifestation, the true idea of all that is—*i.e.* the true idea of all that is permanent. St. Paul pointed out that the Christ, of which, as he showed, your true self is a part, is " *the power of God, and the wisdom of God* " (1 Cor. 1 : 24). St. Paul also said : " *Now ye are the body of Christ, and members in particular* " (1 Cor. 12 : 27). Our Lord, through his wonderful knowledge, as he usually did, put it more strongly than anyone else. As recorded in John 10 : 34, he quoted the 82nd Psalm and said : " *Ye are gods,*" and drove it home by adding, " *and the scripture cannot be broken.*" This is why St. Paul said : " *We are the children of God : and if children, then heirs ; heirs of God, and joint heirs with Christ* " (Rom. 8 : 16, 17). " *In him* [God] *we live, and move, and have our being* " (Acts 17 : 28). In other words, " *God created man in his own image* " (Gen. 1 : 27) ; " *For God created man to be immortal, and made him to be an image of his own eternity* " (Wisdom of Solomon 2 : 23) Man is now, always has been and always will be, a perfect being in a perfect world, governed by a perfect God. " *Whosoever is born of God doth not commit sin* " (1 John 3 : 9). " *For ye are all children of God* " (Gal 3 : 26).

" Ye are of God . . . greater is he that is in you, than he that is in the world " (1 John 4 : 4).

This truth is not new. It is from everlasting to everlasting, and it has come shining through the mist of matter into the world whenever there was anyone sufficiently pure and perfect to teach and demonstrate it. Our Lord was the great example, and he gave the knowledge to mankind, proving it in a way in which no one else has ever done. He was continually demonstrating his knowledge of God. 10

Medical Profession recognizing Mental Healing.

The strides made during the last few years in psychology and true metaphysics have been immense. The medical world, although having not yet found the true method of working, have recognized what is called mental healing. One of the leading medical authorities at the War Office recently stated to the writer that the only word which could be applied to the results now being obtained at the Military Hospitals by mental suggestion, was the one word " miracle." It is true that 20 mental suggestion gives extraordinary results in the direction of the suggestions made, but it is harmful in other respects, and the total result is not beneficial to the patient. For this reason the principal medical authority on the subject, a consulting physician in Harley Street, has, he told me, given it up, after having obtained marvellous results. Still, mental suggestion is a sign of the awakening of the world to the possibility of true mental healing, healing by divine Mind. This the above authority now admits is the only true method of healing. 30

Matter merely Mental Phenomena.

It is now well known that every thought a man thinks is followed by an effect upon himself, more or less, according to the intensity with which he thinks it ; we bring all our troubles upon ourselves by wrong thinking. As Jeremiah said : *" I will bring evil upon this people, even the fruit of their thoughts "* (Jer. 6 : 19). All mental workers and advanced psychologists know to-day that this effect is not limited to oneself, but every thought you think about another person, and every thought you think 40 about matter, is followed by an apparent result, more or

less, in the direction that you are thinking, because matter is merely mental phenomena. As Huxley said, we have to recognize the world of reality (heaven) and the world of phenomena. In other words, the material world is a world of materialized thoughts. Fortunately for the world, there are very few who think so strongly that its apparent effect is noticeable, for, sad to say, most thoughts, until you learn to think rightly, are thoughts of evil or impending evil. All the results obtained by
10 the sorcerers, witches, black and white magic workers, etc., for which there is a mass of evidence, are due to this. Jesus exposed this claim to an apparent power, and five times showed that matter is merely mental phenomena. His first statement to this effect was made after he had healed the lunatic boy, and his disciples asked why they had been unable to heal him, when he said : " Verily I say unto you, If ye have faith as a grain of mustard seed, ye shall say unto this mountain, Remove hence to yonder place ; and it shall remove ; and nothing
20 shall be impossible unto you " (Matt. 17 : 20). It has been thought that this was the method in which they were to pray, but he followed on by saying, " Howbeit this kind goeth not out but by prayer and fasting " (the latter two words, I am told, were added about the fifth century). This shows that he had not healed the demoniac by strong thinking, but by true prayer.

The next is in Matthew 21 : 21, when he said, " If ye have faith, and doubt not, ye shall not only do this which is done to the fig tree, but also if ye shall say unto this
30 mountain, Be thou removed, and be thou cast into the sea ; it shall be done."

Then we come to Mark 9: 23, when Jesus said, "If thou canst believe, all things are possible to him that believeth."

The Greek word " pistis " means " faith founded on knowledge," knowledge of God, not blind belief, but belief in God, good, being the only reality and the only power.

Two chapters later, namely, in Mark 11 : 23—which is
40 practically the same account as that given in Matthew 21, except that in the previous verse, Jesus said to them, " Have faith in God "—we read : " Whosoever shall say unto this mountain, Be thou removed, and be thou cast

*into the sea ; and shall not doubt in his heart, but shall
believe that those things which he saith shall come to pass ;
he shall have whatsoever he saith."*

Verse 24 runs on as follows : " *Therefore I say unto
you, What things soever ye desire, when ye pray, believe
that ye receive them, and ye shall have them.*" In the
revised version the revisers have altered this to, " *All
things whatsoever ye pray and ask for, believe that ye have
received them, and ye shall have them.*" They were
obliged to do this because in every case in the original 10
the word is in the past tense, namely, " *have received.*"
This verse is the key to the miracles of Jesus. It does
not mean think lies and think you have a thing when you
have not got it. It means that when you pray you have
to know that you, the spiritual being, the only you that
there really is, have received, and then you, the material
being, the counterfeit you, are out of your difficulty,
either by having what you desire or by finding that you
do not want it. In the authorized version the translators
altered it because it did not, in their opinion, make sense, 20
or appear to agree with the teachings of Jesus ; but he
did not say we must think lies ; on the contrary, he
said : " *Ye shall know the truth, and the truth shall make
you free*" (John 8 : 32).

When praying in this way we never can be sure of
what will happen, because we can never be certain of
what is best for us. All that you can be sure of is that
good will come to you. "*With God all things are
possible*" (Matt. 19 : 26).

The fifth reference is in Luke 17 : 6, which runs as 30
follows: " *If ye had faith as a grain of mustard seed, ye
might say unto this sycamine tree, Be thou plucked up by
the root, and be thou planted in the sea ; and it should
obey you.*"

There are other instances to be found throughout the
Bible which show that the material world is simply
mental phenomena.

The Mystery of the Material World.

There are three classes of thinkers—the theologians,
the metaphysicians, and the natural scientists. They all 40
have different methods of expressing their views about
the material world, but none of them can say anything

that is true about it. You may call them three authorized classes of liars. They can only say what is correct and accurate, because there is no reality in the material world ; it is only a false concept of the spiritual world, heaven. As it is only a false human concept, this concept varies with your thought and the amount of your faith or strong belief, as our Lord, as I have shown, pointed out five times.

When we want to heal a patient, what has to be healed is our own false concept of God's man. We blaspheme when we say that man is sinning, is in want, or is sick, because we are stating that God has been unable to create man properly. The man that God made is spiritual and perfect. He is now, always has been, and always will be, a perfect being, in a perfect world, made "*in the image of God*" (Gen. 1 : 27), governed by a perfect God.

The Difficulty of Language.

In teaching people how to pray, at the very outset we are met with the difficulty of language. One cannot say anything that is true about evil and the material world, because it does not exist. This means that it has no permanence ; it is only a temporary illusion. Nearly all the great thinkers have taught this. St. Augustine—the founder of the present Christian religion—five times pointed out that evil is not real. Four times he argues it out in the following way :—God made everything very good, evil is not good, therefore God did not make it. God made all things, therefore evil is not real. There is no flaw in this logic if you admit that God made all things. Natural science teaches this. It teaches that there is only one cause ; this cause must be good and can only be known by its manifestation, which must partake of the nature of cause, and be good. This cause is better known by the name of God, who is the cause of all things, and is the only cause.

Ignorance the Cause of all our Troubles.

It is ignorance of the fact that if you think a thing strongly enough it will happen, which has misled the world as to the nature of prayer. It was thought that if one asked God to do something, and then had sufficient faith that it would happen, God heard and acted in accordance with one's faith. It is known now that whether the faith is in God, or in a devil, or in drugs, the result is the same, and that blind faith in God in this way will bring about an evil result just as readily as a good result. Ordinary or supplicatory prayer addressed to a distant unknown potentate, who is implored to alter what is presumed to be in accord with the working of His law, is of necessity erroneous. It may almost be said to be trying to teach God His business. *" For who hath known the mind of the Lord, that he may* 10 *instruct him "* (1 Cor. 2 : 16). The effect is in accordance with the intensity of the human thought ; not that the human thought causes it, but the apparent effect always follows unless destroyed by true prayer.

The only power evil has, is the power we give it in our own mind by thinking of the evil and believing it to be there. The serpent told Eve that if Adam and she ate of the fruit of the trees, *" ye shall be as gods, knowing good and evil "* (Gen. 3 : 5). It is the knowledge of evil that gives us all our troubles. If you can keep the 20 evil thoughts out they cannot act. It is easy to keep an evil thought out of the conscious mind, for instance, by reading an interesting book. The question is, how to keep it out of the subconscious mind. This can only be done by actively thinking of God and of heaven. To do this you must understand, as far as possible, the nature of God.

Solomon makes the ungodly man, when speaking of the righteous man, say : *" He professeth to have the knowledge of God : and he calleth himself the child of* 30 *the Lord. He was made to reprove our thoughts. . . . We are esteemed of him as counterfeits . . . and maketh his boast that God is his father "* (Wisdom of Solomon, 2 : 13–14–16).

It must not be forgotten that in supplicatory prayer, during part of the time one is thinking of God, and whilst so thinking, the action of God takes place. If, for instance, in a man's petition he says, " I pray Thee, Lord, relieve me of this headache, if it be Thy will," when he says, " Lord," the action of God, although it may be 40 scarcely noticeable, does take place, because he is thinking of God. But the words " relieve me of my headache " express a thought which actually is followed by his being worse, because he is thinking of himself as having a headache.

But this is to be remembered, that whereas when he says " relieve me of my headache," it is worse, the harm only takes place *at the time* ; on the other hand, when he turns to God and prays, " I pray Thee, Lord," then for the rest of his existence the severity of all his headaches is permanently diminished, as, for the moment, he is thinking of absolute good, and the human mind cannot
10 get worse. It is always improving slowly ; when you are thinking of God it is improving rapidly.

CHAPTER II

TRUE PRAYER

I F supplicatory prayer is not right, what then is right ? To find this out we have to recognize that although if we think evil, evil follows, yet if we continue by thinking good we undo the harm done and bring about good.

But what is good ?

We have been in the habit of thinking that intel-
20 lectually we could tell what is good for a person. But when a man has sufficient experience, he knows that it is an extremely difficult thing to tell what is best for himself, much less for someone else. Consequently it cannot be right to think strongly that what we believe is good for a person will take place, in order to bring about that particular thing, as we may be badly mistaken. Socrates, one of the first of the ethical mystics, taught that we must not pray for any particular good, but only for good generally.

30 Logically it is clear that if we want to bring about the perfect good, we have to think of the highest good that we can possibly imagine. What is this highest good ? Our Master said, " *Why callest thou me good ? there is none good but one, that is, God* " (Mark 10 : 18), and the only way in which we can be certain of bringing about good is, not by thinking of the material world, and so-called good—as everything in the material world is more or less evil, some so little evil that we call it good—but by thinking of what is called God and heaven ; cause and

its manifestation ; Mind and its ideas. Whatever you may choose to call it, it is a perfect, ideal state of consciousness, a mental world, the realm of infinite, divine Love. *" Look unto me, and be ye saved, all the ends of the earth : for I am God, and there is none else "* (Isa. 45 : 22).

Now we see why the mystics, who, with all their shortcomings, were in many cases wonderful men, living wonderful lives, always impressed upon mankind the necessity for the realization of God, and we learn why such men as Brother Lawrence, and such women as 10 Madame de Guyon, obtained the results they did. Now we see also why St. Paul said : *" I can do all things through Christ "* (Phil. 4 : 13).

Failure of the Mystics to help Others.

Why is it, however, that they were able to help themselves, and yet, apparently, were seldom, if ever, really able to help others, and to free them from sin, disease, and trouble ? The reason is, they did not seem to recognize that things are as we think, and that if it was desired to help somebody else by the realization of God, they had 20 to start by thinking that the action of God was going to take place on the person whom they wanted to help—it is sufficient to have the intention of helping them—then they had to realize God, in just the same way as they had realized God with the object of helping themselves, and of bringing peace of mind and joy into their own hearts.

If they had done this, the action would have been seen in the person whom they wanted to help, and there cannot be any doubt, but that wonderful results would have been obtained, for true prayer is thinking of God, 30 conscious communion with God. It is doubtful, however, whether they would have noticed these wonderful results, because healing by the realization of God, by the affirmation of good, means permanent purification, and therefore healing of the human mind, so that the person can never have any difficulty of the kind again, and it is difficult to do this instantaneously by the affirmation. It is easy to do it by the denial of the evil, the denial of the existence in heaven of the trouble, but the effect is not permanent. It is easy to do it gradually by the 40 affirmation, but this result they might not have recognized as being due to their work. The denial is only temporary relief, yet sometimes of great importance, as when the person is in extreme pain and it takes time to change the mind and free the victim.

Perhaps if they had been persistent and frequent in their endeavours, with the underlying desire to help in some special case, they might have succeeded in obtaining some instantaneous results—even if they had not used the denial—and thus they would have discovered the key to the miracles of Jesus, namely, active Right Thinking 10 or conscious communion with God, with the object of overcoming some specific trouble.

The Conditions of an Ideal World.

We have to think the highest good of which we are capable of thinking. Surely the supreme good is an absolutely perfect mental world where everything is governed by the Principle of good.

Let us consider what should be the conditions in such a mental world. Well, all men must be absolutely loving towards all. There can be no death ; all men must 20 have Life eternal. There can be no want, because directly a man needs anything he must have it ; and when he has it, it must be something that cannot possibly do him any harm, but helps him and gives him joy and happiness. There can be no worry or trouble of any kind ; nothing but joy, bliss, and happiness. There can be no want of knowledge ; man should instantly know everything he needs. There can be no difficulty in going from place to place ; man should be instantly wherever he wishes to be, and when there, he ought to find it an 30 absolutely perfect ideal, mental state, where man should be always enjoying himself, and having lovely ideas of music, art, literature, etc., always coming to him. These ideas should unfold with perfect sequence, being governed by the Principle of law and order. These ideas can never be idle, therefore man must always be utilizing them for the benefit of his fellow-man. One of the great sources of happiness is work, and the feeling that we are doing something of value for others. Man should, therefore, be always intensely active and working 40 perfectly. In this work, as with everything, man must manifest wisdom, intelligence, and knowledge. Naturally, there can be no disease ; man must always be absolutely healthy ; nor can there be any limitations of any kind or description. Of course, such a world should be governed by an ever-active Principle, the Principle of good, and amongst the various things that form the Principle of good, which is always acting in such a perfect world, must be the Principle of love, which is Love itself, and the Principle of life, which is Life itself. Truth must always prevail.

It is quite easy for anyone who has the gift of analytical deduction to think out for himself the details of such an absolutely perfect ideal mental world.

Some of my readers will be astonished to hear that whilst they are doing this, they are praying or, as it is called by the mental workers, treating, because this perfect ideal mental world is what the religious world calls heaven. In other words, it is a perfect state of consciousness which exists now, of which we form an utterly false concept called the material world. The only hell we shall ever be in, we are in now, and we make our own comparative heaven and our own hell by the way in which we think.

CHAPTER III

WATCH AND PRAY

" *AND what I say unto you I say unto all, Watch* " (Mark 13 : 37). These are the last words of Jesus in one of the most important chapters in the Bible, one containing the prophecy of the end of the world.

What is it that we have to watch ? We have to watch our thoughts so as to let no evil thought into our mind, otherwise this evil will be manifested. If you can keep evil out of your mind, it cannot act. The only power it has, is that we give it in our own minds by thinking it. Unfortunately the subconscious mind is the real culprit, and often the trouble is on us, and is, so to speak, intensified by the conscious mind, before we start working to drive the evil thought out.

The First Commandment, Think only of God, good.

If we stop thinking of the evil, we must be thinking of something, and we have to think of good, not the so-

called good, which we call good in this material world, but we have to think of absolute good, namely, of God and of heaven. Think good and you will get good. This is the covenant that Moses described. He made a statement of vital importance when he put into the mouth of God the following words : *" Thou shalt have no other gods before me "* (Ex. 20 : 3). The following verses also have a vital meaning : *" Thou shalt not make unto thee any graven image, or any likeness of any thing that is* 10 *in heaven above, or that is in the earth beneath, or that is in the water under the earth : Thou shalt not bow down thyself to them, nor serve them : for I the Lord thy God am a jealous God, visiting the iniquity of the fathers upon the children unto the third and fourth generation of them that hate me."* It is from failure to carry out this commandment that all our troubles arise. We mentally make our graven image and false likeness of all the spiritual realities in heaven by thinking of the material counterfeits. Solomon makes the wicked man, in speak-
20 ing of the *" righteous "* or right-thinking man, say, *" We are esteemed of him as counterfeits "* (Wisdom of Solomon 2 : 16). Instead, we must always keep our mind, as the prophet Isaiah said, *" stayed on God."* If we did this, then the sixth verse, as follows, would become practical, and God would show *" mercy unto thousands of them that love me, and keep my commandments."*

The " Gospel " or " Good News " of the " Covenant of Salvation."

This covenant of salvation, namely, that if we think
30 good, *i.e.* think of God, we shall obtain good, is referred to right throughout the Bible. In fact, the word " Testament " ought really to be translated " Covenant," which is the true translation. We ought to speak of the " New Covenant " and the " Old Covenant."

The word translated " gospel," as Cruden points out, means " good news " or " glad tidings " of salvation. Cruden states that these glad tidings were the sum of the covenant contained in the promise made to Abraham. Paul says that the Christians of Ephesus *" trusted in*
40 *Christ . . . after that ye heard the word of truth, the gospel of your salvation "* (Eph. 1 : 12–13). This word of truth and gospel, or good news of our salvation, is the

fact that matter is not a reality, and disappears, with all its attendant evils in the shape of sin, disease, limitations, and all other troubles, on the realization that it is not true, as the only reality is God and His manifestation. This is the gospel or good news now coming all over the world for the relief of mankind in these times of stress, and if, when evil attacks, you will realize this clearly enough, it goes at once. Things are as you think, and if you think with sufficient certainty that there is no evil, the evil is gone. We cannot, however, think lies, 10 and therefore what we have to think is that there is no evil *in heaven*, no evil in God's perfect world, where " *God saw everything that he had made, and, behold, it was very good* " (Gen. 1 : 31).

The first verse of Romans runs as follows :—" *Paul, a servant of Jesus Christ, called to be an apostle, separated unto the gospel of God.*" This means that he devoted his life to preaching the gospel, namely, that " *we being many, are one body in Christ* " (Rom. 12 : 5), that is, spiritual beings in heaven, for " *if any man be in Christ,* 20 *he is a new creature* " (2 Cor. 5 : 17). He said : " *the invisible things of him from the creation of the world are clearly seen, being understood by the things that are made* " (Rom. 1 : 20). This means that the spiritual things which we do not see, have always existed, being made by God, and that we clearly understand what the spiritual or heavenly things are like, not through the matter that is around us, and merely hides heaven from us, but on account of these spiritual " *invisible things,*" these heavenly tints that shine through the mist of 30 matter and are seen, although more or less imperfectly.

We must watch and pray without ceasing ; in other words, we must " *look not at the things which are seen, but at the things which are not seen : for the things which are seen are temporal ; but the things which are not seen are eternal* " (2 Cor. 4 : 18). In other words, keep your mind " *stayed on* " God (Isa. 26 : 3). Then the glories of God's perfect world are disclosed to us.

Paul speaks clearly in the 16th verse, where he says, " *For I am not ashamed of the gospel of Christ : for it is* 40 *the power of God unto salvation to every one that be- lieveth.*" This " *gospel of Christ,*" or " good news of Christ," is " *the power of God unto salvation.*" By the realization of the fact that man is a spiritual being in heaven now, the action of God, omnipotence itself, takes place, bringing about "*salvation*" to those who realize it, and ultimately "*salvation*" to the whole world. Then all matter disappears, or as the Bible in many places calls it, "*dissolves*," and we all appear to wake up and see heaven as it really is.

The Everlasting Gospel.

10 In Revelation 14 : 6, we read : "*I saw another angel fly in the midst of heaven, having the everlasting gospel to preach unto them that dwell on the earth, and to every nation, and kindred, and tongue, and people.*" The word "*angels*" is used in the Bible as meaning the thoughts that come to man. Sometimes they are God's angels —high, uplifting thoughts. Sometimes they are devil's angels—evil thoughts. In this case, shortly before the end of all evil, John saw an "*angel fly in the midst of heaven*," namely, an uplifting thought, a spiritual message coming to mankind, pointing out that there is 20 nothing real but God, and God's perfect world, and that all the evil therefore comes from our own wrong thinking. It calls upon mankind to cease thinking the evil, which then is terrible in its attack upon humanity, and to realize that " there is nothing but God." The "*gospel*" is the good tidings or good news that all evil is immediately about to vanish through the widespread realization by mankind that "there is nothing but God." Then even the selfish materialist will do his best, in the hope that it may be true, and that the terrible troubles he has been 30 enduring, and which have been foretold by the prophets throughout the Bible as coming at the so-called end of the world, are about to disappear. Jesus foretold this good news when he said, "*This gospel of the kingdom shall be preached in all the world for a witness unto all nations ; and then shall the end come*" (Matt. 24 : 14).

The recognition that there is no reality in matter and evil, and that God and heaven are around us, perfect and eternal, leads to the time when, "*in such an hour as ye think not, the Son of man cometh*" (Matt. 24 : 44). Then 40 "*the glory of the Lord shall be revealed, and all flesh shall see it together*" (Isa. 40 : 5), with the result that "*God shall wipe away all tears from their eyes ; and there shall be no more death, neither sorrow, nor crying, neither shall there be any more pain : for the former things are passed away* " (Rev. 21 : 4), and we shall see the " *new heavens and a new earth, wherein dwelleth righteousness* " (2 Peter 3 : 13).

The Hidden Mystery Revealed.

In the third chapter of Ephesians, Paul pointed out that he " *was made a minister . . . to make all men see what is the fellowship of the mystery, which from the beginning of the world hath been hid in God* " (Eph. 3 : 7–9). Part of his mission was to make man understand that all are " *in Christ* " ; all are really spiritual beings in heaven, now, part of God's consciousness. This is a mystery to the material man even to-day. He finds it most difficult to understand that the matter we see around us is not real. This mystery is now revealed, as was prophesied in the Apocalypse, where we read, " *in the days of the voice of the seventh angel, when he shall begin to sound, the mystery of God should be finished, as he hath declared to his servants the prophets* " (Rev. 10 : 7). We understand not only the nature of God and His Christ, and what takes place in heaven, but we have grasped, intellectually at all events, that matter is not a reality, but is at best a temporary mental illusion.

Not only do we now understand the nature—called " *name* " in the Bible—of God and His Christ, and what takes place in heaven, but each man can prove it for himself, as, if there is anything wrong in the material world and you realize clearly enough the nature of God and His Christ, the difficulty instantly disappears.

The Second Coming of Christ.

This knowledge of the fact that man is not a material being, liable to sin, disease, and trouble of every kind, but that he is a perfect being in heaven, " *in Christ,*" *i.e.* part of God's consciousness, is the second coming of Christ ; the millennial second coming which like lightning is coming now all over the world. " *As the lightning cometh out of the east, and shineth even unto the west ; so also shall the coming of the Son of man be* " (Matt. 24 : 27). Yet all the leading philosophers have more or less taught that man is not material. Some of them I deal with more fully later on.

What Philosophers have Taught.

Pythagoras taught that man is immortal.

Zeno, whom Aristotle called " the Father of Logic," taught that not only the substance and movement of things, but the movement and change have no real existence of their own, but are merely an illusion of the senses.

Parmenides, one of the great and noble men of the past—for centuries they spoke of Parmidian nobleness—
10 said that the material world is merely " shadowy and illusionary appearances without reality."

Plato taught that our real selves existed in Mind before we, the material beings, were born. He said, " This world which appears to the senses, has no true being," and spoke of its comprehension as more illusion than knowledge.

Plotinus stated that matter is nothing.

Aristotle said that the " nous " of man is eternal and has no birth, whereas the animal soul—the human
20 mind—being acquainted with perishable things, perishes with them.

Euclid said that evil is only an illusion of our sensuous nature, and has no real existence.

Spinoza said that evil has no existence, for God is the only substance.

St. Augustine, the founder of modern Christianity, said that evil is not real.

The early Fathers recognized the non-reality of matter ; for instance, Origen wrote about the year
30 A.D. 125 : " Seeing evil nowhere exists, for God is all things, and to Him no evil is near." Writing of the material he says : " Its mind and hostile will, which come not from God, but from itself, are to be destroyed."

Martin Luther looked upon the material world as an illusion essentially evil and misleading.

Bishop Berkeley, Bishop of Coyne, said : " I deny . . . that there is any material substance." " There is nothing but man's thoughts of things."

The Views of Modern Thinkers.

40 The great Emmanuel Kant said that " this world's life is only an appearance, a sensuous image of the pure spiritual life, and the whole world of sense only a picture

swimming before us like a dream and having no reality in itself."

Fichte said that we are in heaven now.

Huxley, Professor at the Royal College of Surgeons and the Royal Institution, said that we had to recognize the world of reality and the world of phenomena. Of the latter he said : " All that we know about matter is that it is the hypothetical substance of physical phenomena." By this he means the imagined reality of what we see around us. He also said that " the only certainty 10 is the existence of mind."

Herbert Spencer said : " Matter, motion, and force are not reality, but the symbols of reality."

Professor Max Müller said that matter or substance is not something existing by itself.

Fiske, the well-known historian, professor of Philosophy at Harvard and St. Louis, wrote : " Apart from consciousness there is no such thing as matter."

Professor Ostwald, of Leipzig University, said that matter is only something we imagine.   20

Father Tyrrell, the Modernist, said that the goodness and wisdom of this world are but caricatures of the Divine, blasphemous because of their very traces of likeness.

Gladstone stated that all evil and evil beings must ultimately be annihilated.

Heydweiller, a well-known German physicist, proved chemically that matter could be made to cease its existence. We now find that his experiments were correct.

Dr. Le Bon, probably the leading physicist of the 30 last decade, and certainly one of the most up-to-date, writes : " The world constructed with the impressions of our senses is a summary translation, and necessarily a far from faithful one, of the real world which we know not." He also said that " matter, hitherto deemed indestructible, slowly vanishes. Energy is no more indestructible than the matter from which it emanates."

Sir William Crookes, late President of the Royal Society, said that the fatal quality of atomic dissociation appears to be universal. " Physicists were now be- 40 ginning to say that in all probability there was no such thing as matter."

Professor Osborne Reynolds, F.R.S., has proved

mathematically that matter is not real. No one can find a flaw in his mathematical proof.

Professor Richet says: "Every living being was, perchance, a chemical mechanism and nothing more."

Bergson says that we cannot even be sure we possess a consciousness. "I might be a well-constructed automaton."

Dean Inge, in his *Paddock Lecture*, referring to the religious problem of evil, writes as follows: "That problem has been stated once for all in the words of Augustine: 'Either God is unwilling to abolish evil, or He is unable; if He is not willing, He is not good; if He is unable, He is not omnipotent.' No Christian can consent to impale himself on either horn of this dilemma. If God is not perfectly good and also perfectly powerful, He is not God. . . . The only other alternative is to deny, to some degree, the absolute existence of evil."

The following from *Tertium Organum*, a recent scientific work by Ouspensky, formerly Professor of Mathematics at the Petrograd Institute, and Engineer for Roads and Ways to the Russian Government, will show how scientific men are now rapidly coming to the conclusion put forward originally in the first lecture that I gave on the subject, many years ago, and fully set out in *Life Understood*, first published in 1910.

"We perceive reality as though through a narrow slit, and what we are seeing through this slit we call the present; what we did see and now do not see—the past, and what we do not quite see but are expecting—the future.

"And when we shall see or feel ourselves in the world of four dimensions we shall see that the world of three dimensions does not really exist and has never existed: that it was the creation of our own fantasy, a phantom host, an optical illusion, a delusion, anything one pleases excepting only reality."

The Bible View.

It is taught in the Bible in many places. St. Paul states it most clearly: "*If a man think himself to be something, when he is nothing, he deceiveth himself*" (Gal. 7 : 3). He also says: "*The things which are seen are temporal; but the things which are not seen are eternal* " (2 Cor. 4 : 18). It is a scientific axiom that anything which ceases to exist is not real now.

In the Book of Isaiah we read : " *Behold, ye are of nothing, and your work of nought* " (Isa. 41 : 24). " *All her princes shall be nothing* " (Isa. 34 : 12). 1 Cor. 11 : 6 shows what the princes are. They are " *the princes of this world, that come to nought.*"

The following are also instructive : " *As for the other people which also come of Adam, thou hast said that they are nothing* " (1 Esdras 6 : 56). " *All nations before him are as nothing; and they are counted to him less than nothing* " (Isa. 40 : 17). Nebuchadnezzar saw this, and said, " *All the inhabitants of the earth are reputed as nothing* " (Dan. 4 : 35). Like that wonderful man Pythagoras, Nebuchadnezzar gained his knowledge from Daniel.

It is the knowledge of God, of absolute good, that we need. It is the knowledge of God that will save us. This knowledge has now come to mankind. " *It shall be said in that day, Lo, this is our God ; we have waited for him, and he will save us* " (Isa. 25 : 9).

" The Mystery of Iniquity doth Already Work."
(2 Thess. 2 : 7).

Metaphysics unlocked the door and gave us the necessary knowledge that God and His manifestation is All-in-all, and that matter is not real, but at best false mental phenomena ; those hypnotically inclined, however, used the latter part of this knowledge wrongly, harming themselves and others.

Natural science, fortunately, is coming to the rescue. In Rev. 12 : 16, we read : " *the earth helped the woman, and the earth opened her mouth, and swallowed up the flood which the dragon cast out of his mouth.*" About eighteen years ago, it came to me that this meant that the earth, namely, the scientific world, would help the woman, and would swallow up the flood which the dragon cast out of his mouth. This is the flood of mental working with the human mind, hypnotism with its admittedly evil brethren, black magic, witchcraft, etc., which would have swallowed up the spiritual teachings that are now coming to save the world, if it had not been for natural science, called in the Bible " *the earth,*" pointing out clearly the difference between the right and wrong methods of prayer.

It is so much easier for those materially minded to learn how to effect apparent miracles with the human mind, either by hypnotism or mental suggestion, than it is to learn how to do them spiritually by the realization of God. *" The natural man receiveth not the things of the Spirit of God : for they are foolishness unto him : neither can he know them, because they are spiritually*
10 *discerned "* (I Cor. 2 : 14). Fortunately those materially minded can only do so-called miracles in the wrong way if they have an hypnotic class of mind. Natural science points out the scientific difference between the two methods of working and, like a policeman, is holding up its hand as a danger signal to those inclined to travel along the wrong road, the road that leads to mental disaster, working with the human mind in order to bring about what one thinks is good.

The " Woman " the Spiritual Idea.

20 *The " woman,"* according to the most advanced meta-physical teacher, symbolizes generic man, the spiritual idea of God. John, in Rev. 12 : 1, saw the spiritual idea as a woman clothed with the sun. The female, as opposed to the male, stands for love, refinement, intuition, and purity. The male qualities are moral courage, strength of character, wisdom, and frankness.

This verse is one of the various places where John gives the position in the heavens of the planets at the time, I believe, of which he was prophesying. It runs
30 as follows :—*" And there appeared a great wonder in heaven ; a woman clothed with the sun, and the moon under her feet, and upon her head a crown of twelve stars."* The *" woman clothed with the sun "* is Virgo in " the house of the Sun " ; the moon is below Virgo and over her head is the constellation known as " the Crown of Twelve Stars." I believe this will be found to be the position of these planets at the exact date of the events prophesied in that chapter. Chapter 14 is a prophecy of what is going to take place during the last week of the
40 material world, and I should not be surprised if the first verse of this chapter, which mentions the *" Lamb,"* or the constellation " Aries," gives the actual position of

various planets and therefore the actual date of the events
prophesied. I do not know enough of astronomy to
know either the names of the other planets referred to or
the date when they will be in the position shown. Perhaps
some astrological reader will give me this information.
There is no doubt that the date of the end of the world,
that is the end of all matter and its resultant evil, is
prophesied in the Bible within a week or so, as there are
quite a number of passages referring to it. The following passages show it : 1 Thess. 5 : 4 ; Rev. 22 : 6 ; 10
2 Peter 1 : 19 ; Isa. 41 : 22 ; Dan. 8 : 19 and 11 : 35 ;
Acts 17 : 31 ; and John 16 : 13–23–24. We shall not,
however, know the actual day and the hour as Jesus
pointed out in Mark 13 : 32, as follows : *" But of that day
and that hour knoweth no man, no, not the angels which are
in heaven, neither the Son, but the Father."* This means
that a man cannot calculate the absolute date of the end,
either mathematically or astrologically ; he cannot tell it
inspirationally by true prayer, namely, by the denial and
affirmation, the angels Michael and Gabriel ; Jesus him- 20
self did not know it, as it depends entirely upon the
action of God and how people then pray.

It is clear that if, to obtain benefits for ourselves or
others, we have to think of good, then this good should
be the highest good that we can possibly imagine, namely,
God and heaven. It is equally clear that we ought continually, throughout the twenty-four hours, to be thinking of God and heaven, thinking of an ideal world, the
most perfect world we can imagine. Unfortunately this
is impossible for a material being, but we should do it as 30
far as possible ; Paul has said, *" For the good that I
would I do not : but the evil which I would not, that I do "*
(Rom. 7 : 19). If a man could reverse all the wrong
thoughts that come to him and continually think of the
world of reality, God and heaven, he would soon cease
to sin, and a little later on would dematerialize and
disappear from the sight of material beings, appearing
to wake up and find himself to be what he really is
now, namely, a perfect spiritual being in an absolutely
perfect world, in heaven. 40

The Natural Science View.

We can look at the material world from the meta-

physical, scientific, or religious points of view. From the scientific point of view, thought is a high tension current right above the Marconi wave, and the human mind is an electrical transmitter, vibrating with these thoughts. Every sin and every disease has its own cell, or, as it has been called metaphysically, " court of consciousness," in the subconscious mind. If the anger cell is clean, a million people could not hypnotize you to be angry, but if there are small electrical particles on the cell,
10 they damp it down, as pitch does a tuning-fork, so that it vibrates with a lower note. In the same way the cell is damped down by the electrical particles, so that every time an angry thought passes over the cell, the cell will vibrate and the man be angry. So-called good thoughts are high vibrations, bad thoughts low vibrations. With the denial, namely, the denial of the existence of the evil in heaven, comes only temporary relief, as it is merely the short-circuiting of the angry thoughts. This is called the angel Michael, which, John shows, destroys
20 the devil's angels, the evil thoughts which attack humanity. The affirmation, or the realization of the perfection of God and heaven, brings about the permanent purification of the mind, the short-circuiting of the particles on the anger cell in the subconscious mind. This is the angel Gabriel, which gives us knowledge, etc. If you can get your realization of God and heaven clear enough, you can never be angry again, as all the particles will be short-circuited and the so-called mind completely purified. From a natural science point of view, the
30 anger cell will not then vibrate with the lower vibrations of angry thoughts.

All Troubles come from Blasphemy.

All our troubles come from two forms of blasphemy. The first form of blasphemy is very simple to understand. We believe that God made man and that He is our Father, " *My Father, and your Father ;* . . . *my God, and your God* " (John 20 : 17), and yet a man practically says, God made me so badly that I have always a headache, or am hard-up, or have a bad temper, etc. The
40 punishment always fits the crime. When we think that we are ill, or that somebody else is ill, or that there is something wrong with the world, things are a little worse ;

whereas, when we stop blaspheming and know that all is spiritual and perfect, some of the imaginary mist of matter in front of heaven, the world of reality, thins and disappears, and we see heaven more as it really is.

The second form of blasphemy is not quite so easy to understand, yet it is quite as bad. The material man cannot do anything that is good. Only the spiritual man is good. *" They that are in the flesh cannot please God "* (Rom. 8 : 8). *" Whosoever is born of God doth not commit* 10 *sin "* (1 John 3 : 9). The whole of the material man's troubles come from blasphemy, setting himself up in opposition to God. All advanced workers now know that the only thinker, the only actor, and the only creator is God. *" I can of mine own self do nothing "* (John 5 : 30), and yet the material man says, " I think," " I do," and even " I create." It is difficult to imagine much worse blasphemy than this, for, as has been pointed out, he does not do any of these things at all. *" For I know that in me dwelleth no good thing "* (Rom. 7 : 10). He is 20 merely, at best, a series of cinema pictures that do not move ; even the apparent thinking is merely the result of a succession of pictures with certain vibrations on each successive picture, which results in the appearance of a man, apparently speaking, thinking, etc. Henri Bergson has pointed out that he cannot prove that the material man has consciousness. He says : " I might be a well-constructed automaton going, coming, speaking— without internal consciousness." This is correct. Where we say that we think, act, or create, it is all 30 blasphemy, breaking the commandments, setting our- selves up in opposition to God, and being punished for it.

Breaking the First Commandment.

We are always breaking the first commandment : *" Thou shalt have no other gods but me "* (Ex. 20 : 3). *" Put not your trust in princes, nor in the son of man, in whom there is no help "* (Ps. 146 : 3). Moses pointed out that if we had many gods we would have many evils, and the whole of our troubles come from giving to evil 40 power in our own minds. We have many gods and many evils.

Breaking the Second Commandment.

We are also continually breaking the second commandment : "*Thou shalt not make unto thee any graven image*" (Ex. 20 : 4). We are continually making graven images, the likeness of the spiritual things. "I made that box," "that is my child"; whereas they are only "*graven images*," false concepts of the world of reality. God is the only thinker, speaker, hearer, actor, lover, and creator, and He does all this by means of man, the real
10 spiritual man, made in God's image and likeness.

"Watch and Pray" and "Pray without Ceasing."

"*Watch ye and pray*" (Mark 14 : 38), "*Pray without ceasing*" (1 Thess. 5 : 17), "*Continue in prayer and watch*" (Col. 4 : 2), clearly mean that we must continually be watching all the thoughts that come to us in order to reverse any wrong thoughts that attack us, so ceasing blaspheming and stopping the evil being done thereby, using the evil thoughts as signposts to turn us back in thought to God. We should then dwell upon God
20 and God's world as long as possible, as our progress depends solely upon the number of seconds throughout the twenty-four hours in which we are thinking of God and of heaven. This is why the prophet Isaiah said that we should keep our minds "*stayed on*" God (Isa. 26 : 3).

The nature of evil is to destroy itself, and by utilizing the evil that comes to us as a spur to Right Thinking, we are constantly realizing the real world, namely, God and heaven. In this way the evil brings about its own destruction, and we are not only permanently helping
30 ourselves, but we are doing good all around us. If the thought comes into your mind, for instance, "how terribly angry that man is," seven times out of ten the man is more angry. If, on the contrary, we turn to heaven and know the truth, that is, realize that there is no anger in heaven, and follow on by thinking of the opposite, for instance, of the absolute love and peace that there is in heaven, then not only have we helped the man temporarily by the denial, but by the affirmation we have helped him and ourselves permanently to be more loving
40 and less susceptible to angry thoughts. The denial is only temporary relief, the affirmation is the permanent purification of the human mind.

The Denial and Affirmation.

The importance of the denial and affirmation is shown by the references to it throughout the Bible. It is spoken of as " *the lesser light* " and " *the greater light* " in Gen. 1 : 16 ; as " *thy rod and thy staff they comfort me* " (Ps. 23 : 4) ; as " *As many as I love, I rebuke and chasten* " (Rev. 3 : 19) ; cause to deny and affirm. To rebuke comes from *re*=again and *bouquer*=to stop. The meaning, according to the Standard Dictionary, is " a strong expression of disapproval, as by one in authority, directed to the offender's sense of morality or justice ; a forcible personal reprimand." It is the word of authority, " *Get thee behind me, Satan* " (Matt. 16 : 23), the denial of the existence of the evil. Then it disappears. " *At thy rebuke they fled* " (Ps. 104 : 7). To chasten, the same dictionary says, is " to make chaste or pure." It come sfrom the Latin word *castigare*= to purify. " *Whom the Lord loveth he chasteneth* " (Heb. 12 : 6). The affirmation in other words is the purification of the so-called human or carnal mind. The denial and affirmation are also spoken of as the Angel Michael which destroys Satan and Satan's angels (Rev. 12 : 7), and the Angel Gabriel which came to Daniel (Dan. 8 : 16 ; 9 : 21), and to Ezra (2 Esdras 4 : 1 ; 7 : 1 ; 10 : 29), to give them knowledge. The denial is the destruction of the evil thoughts, Satan's angels, and it is through the affirmation that one gains knowledge ; by the realization, for instance, that " God is Truth and man knows Truth."

The importance of the denial and affirmation is shown when, in the sermon on the mount, Jesus said, " *Let your conversation be, Yea, yea ; Nay, nay : for whatsoever is more than these cometh of evil* " (Matt. 5 : 37) ; in other words, whenever you are thinking of anything but of heaven, you are thinking of the material world which is more or less always evil, and evil follows. " *Yea, yea,*" is the affirmation, and " *Nay, nay,*" is the denial. Whenever you are denying and affirming you are thinking of heaven, and so-called good follows, namely, the mist of matters thins and less evil is seen.

Reverse Every Wrong Thought. 40

Every thought unlike God has to be reversed. If you see somebody crying, turn to heaven and realize that there is no such thing as misery in that perfect world, and then think of the opposite, think of the absolute joy, happiness, and bliss that the real man perpetually experiences.

When somebody tells you that their child is always telling lies, turn to heaven and realize as clearly as you possibly can that God's man never lies; for God is Truth, and man is made in His image and likeness, therefore man is absolutely truthful. If you can get a really clear realization of this as a fact, the child will never lie again, the human so-called mind of the child having been permanently purified in this respect. We must not allow ourselves even to think of the material man. We then are thinking of evil, of something that is not good, not absolutely good, and evil invariably follows. This is why St. Paul says, " *Henceforth know we no man after the flesh* " (2 Cor. 5 : 16).

So every wrong thought and every false sense of every kind has immediately to be reversed. Fortunately this is the only thing you have to trouble about. " *Watch and pray* " and " *pray without ceasing* "; use every wrong thought as a signpost to turn you back in thought to God. Whilst we are working in this way, the action of God is taking place, continually purifying our so-called minds. This is dwelling " *in the secret place of the most High* " (Ps. 91 : 1), this is entering " *into thy closet* " (Matt. 6 : 6), this is getting on " *the high mountain* " (Isa. 40 : 9). When Jesus went on to the mountain to pray, he did not necessarily go on to a material mountain. The " *mountain* " symbolically means the uplifted thought. This is why in Psalm 43 : 3 we read: " *O send out thy light and thy truth : Let them lead me ; let them bring me unto thy holy hill.* " And in Psalm 121 : 1-2 : " *I will lift up mine eyes unto the hills from whence cometh my help. My help cometh from the Lord.* "

This is the only thing worth doing in this material world, and is true prayer, namely, active, conscious communion with God.

CHAPTER IV

DENY THYSELF AND FOLLOW ME

Deny that You are Material.

JESUS said, "*If any man will come after me, let him deny himself, and take up his cross daily, and follow me*" (Luke 9 : 23). We used to think that this meant we had to give up many of the things we liked, and make the best of our troubles.

"*Deny*" thyself really means that we have to deny that we are material and realize that we are spiritual. St. Paul said : "*For if a man think himself to be something, when he is nothing, he deceiveth himself*" (Gal. 6 : 3). A man told me that in the British Museum he had found some writings in Latin recording conversations between Jesus and John, believed to be the ancient records of the African Church, and authentic. In one conversation John asks Jesus if there is a material body. Jesus answers "No." John then asks Jesus if there is a material earth, a material creation. Jesus again replies "No." The British Museum authorities know nothing of these records. The statements, however, are absolutely correct. I would be glad to have the reference to them.

"*Take up his cross daily*" means that we have to pray daily and deal mentally, by true prayer, with every difficulty.

"*Follow me*" means that we have to follow him in thought to God. Then one by one we deny the existence of our difficulties, and after each denial add a series of affirmations, the opposites of the trouble the existence of which in heaven we have denied.

When we then dwell upon the perfection of God's perfect world, the mist of matter thins and the human mind improves, "*While we look not at the things which are seen, but at the things which are not seen, for the things which are seen are temporal ; but the things which are not seen are eternal*" (2 Cor. 4 : 18). The statement that "*the things which are seen are temporal*" is St. Paul's statement that they are not real. Scientifically we know that anything which ceases to exist is not real whatever it may appear to be.

At one time there was a group of mental workers in England calling themselves Divine Scientists. Their method of working was to keep all the evil thoughts out of their minds, as far as they could, by not thinking of them, and to dwell in thought on the good of the real world. Merely not thinking of the troubles is useless; it is the denial of their existence that is needed to give the temporary relief which is necessary, whilst by the affirmation we permanently change the mind so that the wrong
10 thoughts have no effect.

Realization of God the only Permanent Healing.

These Divine Scientists did not get on very well, because, as I have pointed out, if a person is healed by the realization of God, by the affirmation of the highest possible good, this means that the cell in the subconscious mind that is liable to vibrate with the evil thoughts, the cause of the trouble, is completely purified, and will not vibrate again with the thoughts, however often they come, and however intense they may be. To do this is
20 not easy, and some time will often elapse before any noticeable results are obtained. Usually people get tired of waiting for results when they are trying a new method of healing, and think that it is of no use unless they feel a benefit almost immediately.

The Denial only Temporary Relief.

The denial of the existence of the evil in heaven being mere temporary relief—the destruction of the thoughts that at the time are attacking—it is very easy to heal a person with the denial, so that they are quite
30 well for the time being.

About a year or so ago a patient came to me who had a bad growth, one of the rare forms, and it had pushed the eye right out of place. She had been operated upon twice, and the surgeons could hold out no hope of any relief from another operation.

A friend of hers had been healed by prayer, and she came and asked whether I would take her as a patient. I said that I would if she would give up the use of the material remedies she was then taking. She said she
40 could not do this. She had not sufficient faith in God, and still believed in matter. I then told her that under these circumstances I could not take her as a patient.

It may be said : " This was rather cruel, was it not ? " No, we have to consider what our object is. It is the reduction of as much as possible of the evil that is going to attack humanity between now and the so-called end of the world, which is the end of all matter and its brood of sin, disease, suffering, and limitations. To do this we have to give as many people as possible such an understanding of the truth, that they themselves can commence not only to get themselves well and happy, but to free those around them from their troubles. 10

When one takes a patient, this is the main object ; although, unless you heal them of the troubles for which they come for help, they, in some cases, are not sufficiently interested to work hard enough to obtain such a knowledge of Truth that they can help others or even themselves.

It is almost impossible to tell who are ready, and who are not ready. A rough method of judging is whether they are willing to pay for the help they obtain, either by a monetary payment or by doing something themselves to help others. Those who are not willing even to give 20 up their material remedies are certainly not sufficiently ready for Truth themselves to make it worth while taking them as patients, unless the worker is not fully occupied with work himself. In the latter event one can work chiefly so that the patient should gain sufficient knowledge of Truth to give up remedies and rely upon God.

I explained this to her, and told her that I had far more patients coming to me than I could possibly take, and, therefore, I could not help her.

She had been in terrible pain for a long time, and was 30 in such agony at the moment, that I said I would give her a treatment against this. Three days afterwards she called again, and said that she had had absolutely no pain whatsoever for two and a half days after the treatment had been given, but that it had come back about twelve hours before, just as badly as ever.

She was, however, sufficiently satisfied by this proof of the existence of God, and said that she would now be quite willing to give up all material remedies, and rely solely upon prayer for her healing, as the doctors had 40 been unable to relieve the pain. I think it required six treatments before the eye was back in position, and about another six treatments before she was well enough to be taken by one of my assistants. She had no pain from the time I gave her the second treatment, and before long one could hardly see that anything had been the matter with her eye at all.

In this case, it was the denial of the existence of pain —in heaven—when I gave the first treatment, which resulted in the thoughts causing the pain to cease for over two days ; but it took more work before the mind was sufficiently changed by the affirmations so that no pain 10 thoughts could again touch her. In the meantime the use of the denial prevented her from feeling any pain, the pain thoughts being destroyed from day to day.

Daily Prayer.

One should treat for oneself regularly twice a day, morning and evening, just in the way that in the old days we used to pray morning and evening, for treatment is merely true prayer. But, whereas in the old days we used to think that five or six minutes was quite sufficient, it will be found that one ought to treat for oneself at 20 least a quarter of an hour each time. Praying regularly in this way enables a man more easily to reverse the wrong thoughts as they come into his mind.

About fourteen or fifteen years ago, when I was being malpractised on, as it is called, by the so-called Christian Scientists, I used to have to pray for myself for five or six hours regularly every night. This was in addition to working as a rule for ten or twelve others every day. The effect of this was that I never suffered in any way, never even having as much as a headache worth speaking 30 of. I thought that I had to protect myself against their evil thoughts. I know now that all that I had to protect myself from was my own wrong thoughts, thinking they could harm me ; whereas there is no power but that of God. The result of the attack was merely that I was helped to obtain a better knowledge of God and to lead a better life. This constant prayer, day after day, means a wonderful purification of the mind, so that evil can have comparatively little effect afterwards.

The Results of Right Thinking.

40 **The first result** of learning how to think rightly, how to pray in the way taught and demonstrated by Jesus

the Christ, is that we find an easy, scientific, and therefore certain method of getting rid of sin out of ourselves.
"*The Lord shall deliver me from every evil work*"
(2 Tim. 55 : 18). Jesus pointed out that it was due to
the action of the Holy Ghost that "*the prince of this world
is judged*" (John 16 : 11). When a man sees, for instance, an angry man, and turns in thought to heaven
and realizes that there is no anger, and thinks of the love
in heaven, he is judging; that is to say, he separates the
evil from the good in his mind, in the way that a judge 10
does in considering evidence. "*He that is spiritual
judgeth all things*" (1 Cor. 2 : 15), namely, reverses every
wrong thought. "*For the time is come that judgment
must begin at the house of God*" (1 Peter 4 : 17). The
result of this judging, or reversing the wrong thoughts, is
that the evil thoughts making the man angry cease their
apparent existence and the man stops being angry.
Judgment is therefore the destruction of evil and in some
half of the passages in the Bible where the word occurs
it is used with this meaning.   20

Secondly.—If you get your realization clear enough
you can heal a man instantaneously of any kind of
sin and disease. "*He sent his word and healed them*"
(Ps. 107 : 20). The "*word*" is the statements of Truth
which come to us when we form a better concept of God's
ideas which are coming to our spiritual selves.

"*Whose soever sins ye remit, they are remitted unto
them.*" The verse continues : "*and whose soever sins ye
retain, they are retained*" (John 20 : 23). This means
that when we see a man sinning it is our false concept 30
of God's man. We are sinning because we "*retain*"
the sin in our mind. We are blaspheming. If we stop
our blasphemy and know the truth clearly enough "*that
whosoever is born of God sinneth not . . . that wicked
one toucheth him not*" (2 John 5 : 18), instantly he stops
sinning.

Thirdly.—You can get yourself or anyone else out of
any trouble under the sun. "*Seek ye first the kingdom
of God ; and all these things shall be added unto you*"
(Luke 12 : 31). Think only of the world of reality. It 40
is only a question then of how soon the trouble disappears.
Every time you reverse your thought there is a permanent
improvement in the so-called human or carnal mind,

which is then less susceptible to the thoughts causing the trouble. " *The eternal God is thy refuge, and underneath are the everlasting arms* " (Deut. 33 : 27).

Fourthly.—Sooner or later, you must obtain perfect peace of mind and happiness ; for " *to be spiritually minded is life and peace* " (Rom. 8 : 6). You will then understand the meaning of the words : " *The peace of God which passeth all understanding* " (Phil. 4 : 7).

CHAPTER V

HOW TO PRAY

One Method of Starting Treatment.

I N starting a treatment it is a good thing to think of God in His various aspects. " *Acquaint now thyself with him, and be at peace : thereby good shall come unto thee* " (Job 22 : 21). Think, therefore, of God as inexhaustible, perfect Love ; incorporeal, everlasting Life ; and ever-present omnipotent Truth, unfolding its own immortal ideas ; as self-existent, unfathomable Mind, which gives all the mental activity in heaven ; divine and sinless Soul, which gives all the wonderful wisdom and knowledge the real man has ; supreme, infinite Spirit, which is the cause of all the goodness and holiness (remember that holiness means wholeness, or perfection) ; divine substance, which gives permanence to everything in the spiritual world ; the unerring and only intelligence ; and last, but not least, as Principle, the Principle of peace, joy, harmony, energy, activity, the Principle of law and order, and the Principle of all the many qualities which, with the main eight qualities already mentioned, make up absolute good, known as God. We should keep our thoughts as far as possible " *stayed on* " God (Isa. 26 : 3). Try to think of yourself always as in the presence of God. " *My presence shall go with thee, and I will give thee rest* " (Ex. 33 : 14).

In commencing your treatment you can think of God as a vast infinite Mind ; in that Mind is the consciousness by means of which God thinks ; that consciousness is as infinite as Mind. Everywhere Mind is, consciousness is ; that consciousness is man specifically, that is to say, all the spiritual beings in heaven. We are all part of that consciousness by means of which God knows and thinks and works. Paul called this the Christ, and spoke of " *Christ the power of God, and the wisdom of God* " (1 Cor. 1 : 24). Using this as a part of the treatment gives you a better idea of what man is.

Then you can think of the infinite ideas circulating in that infinite Mind, being passed from man to man by the action of God as Love. In addition, man groups together God's ideas into glorious combinations. Some of them 10 we call in the material world a sonata, a poem, a literary gem. He then calls your attention to this perfect combination, that is, passes it on to you. You receive it, and rejoice in it, and obtain also the joy from perceiving the joy he has in giving it to you. Then you in your turn pass it on to others, and obtain the joy from the recognition of their happiness.

Think of Infinity.

Next you can think of the infinite Life, infinite Love, infinite Truth, infinite intelligence, joy, wisdom, and 20 beauty, etc., in that perfect world. In treatment, whenever you can put in the word " infinite," do so. This gets you away from the limitations of legs and arms and shapes and forms, and broadens your thought of God and heaven. Heaven is a world of four dimensions, of which we see three. The fourth dimension is infinity, which swallows up the limitations of length, breadth, and height. In other words, heaven is a dimensionless world, a perfect state of consciousness.

In heaven everything is infinite. You have existed 30 for infinite time ; you have known an infinite number of spiritual beings, every one of them different, every one of them perfect. Every spiritual being reflects infinite Love, Life, wisdom, joy, knowledge, and beauty, and yet he has his individuality, which consists of the different combinations of ideas, the ideas of art, literature, music, scenery, etc., which each individual spiritual being presents to you to give you joy and happiness therefrom. You have been to infinite spiritual worlds, every one of them different, every one of them perfect. Of them we 40 can now photograph about 400 million misrepresentations in the form of the stars. You have heard infinite sonatas,

symphonies, poems, literary gems, etc., every one different, and every one perfect, and you yourself have
created an infinite number, every one of them different,
and every one of them perfect, because God creates
by means of the spiritual beings in heaven, called by
St. Paul "*the Christ.*" Each spiritual being is as perfect
as every other spiritual being and in infinite time has
created an infinite number of everything which God
creates.   God as Life, brings you the ideas ;   God as
10 Truth, enables you to understand them ;   God as Love,
causes you to pass them on.   The "*Logos,*" or "*Word,*"
is the creative action of God which causes man to create
everything that God creates.   God never created the
ideas, and never created man.   They always have existed,
perfect, otherwise at one time God would not have been
complete.   The only things that are created, or ever
have been created, are the infinite combinations of ideas
which God is always creating and has always been
creating by means of man.

20   Then having started your treatment by getting as
clear an idea of heaven, the realm of Mind, as possible,
keep dwelling in thought on this perfect world until you
have finished treating for yourself or for your patient,
as the case may be.

Work against Details at present Necessary.

Before you start to work against the details of the
troubles you want to overcome, it is better to work
against the main evils.   Working against the main evils,
and also against the detailed troubles, is like using a
30 double-barrelled gun, one barrel of which is rifled for
a bullet.

Working against the main evils is like using the shot-
gun : it is bound to hit somewhere or other, although it
may not be so effective as working definitely against the
various symptoms of the trouble.   This, like using the
rifled barrel, is very effective if you hit the mark.

I always myself start by working against universal
evil.   This is called the devil in theology, the ether by
scientific men, and mortal mind by the modern schools of
40 mental healing.   Then I work against thoughts of *materia
medica*, namely, false medical beliefs ; for instance, that
because you catch measles you are bound to be ill for a

certain time ; scarlet fever a different length of time ; that certain foods produce indigestion ; if you cut an artery you must bleed to death, etc. Then I work against fear, which John speaks of in Revelation 21 : 8, when he writes : *" But the fearful, and unbelieving, and the abomin- able, and murderers, and whoremongers, and sorcerers, and idolaters, and all liars, shall have their part in the lake which burneth with fire and brimstone : which is the second death."* This is the death of matter and its attendant evils. This is the only thing that dies.   10

The end of all matter and of the material man is dematerialization. The word *" dissolve "* is used in the Bible, when dematerialization, or the disappearance for ever of all matter is spoken of. In the account that our Lord gives of the end of the world, he ends up as follows : *" Then shall two be in the field ; the one shall be taken, and the other left "* (Matt. 24 : 40). In the account in Luke 17 : 34, 35, it is still more exact, because it says : *" There shall be two men in one bed,"* and *" Two women shall be grinding together ; the one shall be taken and the* 20 *other left."* This means that the material man will be taken and the spiritual man alone will remain ; in other words, the mist of matter will disappear and everyone will appear to wake up and find themselves what they always have been, perfect spiritual beings, in a perfect world, governed by a perfect God.

Fear can be Utilized.

John puts fear first, because fear is a belief in a power other than that of God, a belief in the power of evil, blasphemy. Fear, however, when a man knows how to 30 pray properly, can be made of actual value by its reversal, because fear is your mental perception of the thoughts that are attacking you at the moment, or are going to attack you in the future, and it shows you in which direc- tion you have to work. If by prayer you can drive out all thoughts of fear, then you know that the difficulty is overcome. It means that the thoughts causing the fear are destroyed, and you are free, at all events, for the time.

Work to Improve your Mind.

Besides working *against* the main troubles you want 40 to work *for* the principal things ; for instance, for love, spiritual perception, and wisdom. We all desire to be more thoughtful and considerate for others : to understand God, Truth better ; to be wiser when trying to help our fellow-men.

In working for a thing it is better to start by thinking of God. For instance, in trying to eliminate anger, irritability, and annoyance, that is, to show more love, start by thinking of God as Love ; then think of Love as omnipotent in the world of reality, acting everywhere and upon everything ; then think of man, the infinite consciousness of God, as being absolutely loving towards all. You must not exactly think of somebody doing something towards another, but think of the absolutely infinite, perfect Love that one being manifests towards another spiritual being, and how this Love is manifested by the passing on of the perfect ideas, which give absolute joy and happiness to all concerned. Dwelling thus on Love and its manifestation, is the opening of the human mind, and, speaking from a theological point of view, allowing the action of God to take place on the necessary portion of the human mind of the patient, so that it is purified, more or less, and does not in the future respond quite so easily to the thoughts which are the opposite of Love, but on the contrary, is acted upon by the loving thoughts.

In working for spiritual perception, I commence by thinking of God as Spirit, the Principle of all goodness and holiness and purity, and then I realize that man has spiritual perception, that is to say, has the power of perceiving perfectly all the spiritual ideas in heaven. I usually continue by realizing that man has spiritual discernment, knows Truth, and is always thinking rightly. The realization of this, results in the improvement of the material man's mind in these respects, so that he can understand spiritual things better. In working for wisdom I realize that God is the Principle of all wisdom, and therefore man reflects divine wisdom, intelligence, and knowledge, and knows instantly everything he needs.

Work against your Difficulties One by One.

I have already pointed out that the words of Jesus, " *If any man will come after me, let him deny himself, and take up his cross daily, and follow me* " (Luke 9 : 23), mean that we have to deny that we are material, turn in thought to God, and daily take up and work against our difficulties. I think that we should take up each of our difficulties one by one, and while still thinking of heaven, deny the existence of the first trouble, and then realize as clearly as we can the existence of the perfection of the opposite *in heaven*. For instance, supposing your difficulty is one of the commonest, namely, not having sufficient to live on comfortably. You would realize that " there is no want, God is the source of all supply, and man has instantly everything he needs." The reason for this is that the only thing man needs in heaven is the ideas of God that continually come to him. You can therefore continue realizing that " there are infinite ideas available to man instantly ; idea after idea follows with perfect regularity." Then, if you have reason to think that your work from which you get your income is not quite satisfactory, to get better work you can realize that " man does perfect work, always passing on these ideas to his fellow-man ; man groups these ideas together into glorious combinations, which radiate out in infinite Mind, giving infinite joy and happiness." You can follow on by realizing that " there is no mortal mind to stop this perfect action, for there is only one Mind, God ; God is the only power and the only ruler."

The secret of overcoming want is the secret of overcoming any form of evil which is constantly coming into your mind. It is to nip the sentence in the bud before it is even completed in your mind. When, for instance, you are going to think, " I shall never be able to pay that bill," before you get further than " I shall never," start your reversal ; for instance, " It is a lie ; man is spiritual and has everything he needs directly it is needed."

In working against specific troubles, say, for instance, against a headache, if you know what the apparent cause of the headache is, you will get rid of it more quickly by denying the existence of its apparent cause. For instance, it may be caused by a fall ; it may be that you think somebody is thinking too strongly about you ; it may be that it comes from bad digestion. In fact, there may be many different apparent causes of a headache. None of them, however, are correct, as there is no cause and effect in the material world. The only cause is God.

The mere detail of the words or, indeed, the detail of what you think, is not of very much importance. The whole object in treatment is to get right away from the material world, so that you are actively thinking of God and of heaven ; then if you have formed an idea of what is going on in heaven, it is easier to continue dwelling on the perfection of that perfect world than if you did not know what was taking place.

Treatment only a Sign of the Healing.

10   When you think of the world of reality it is only a sign, but an infallible sign, that the so-called healing is taking place, that the imaginary mist of matter which hides heaven from us, is thinning and disappearing, so that we see heaven more and more as it is, a man as well instead of ill, happy instead of miserable. Man's progress depends solely upon the number of seconds during the twenty-four hours in which he is thinking of God and His wonderful world, heaven. The Prophet Isaiah says : " *Thou wilt keep him in perfect peace, whose mind is*
20 *stayed on thee* " (Isa. 26 : 3). By steadily working in this way, your knowledge of God grows, and as it grows, so it becomes easier and easier to get right away from all thoughts of the material world, until at last all thoughts of sin, disease, and limitations disappear, and you appear to find yourself in God's perfect world. " *Ye shall seek me, and find me, when ye shall search for me with all your heart* " (Jer. 29 : 13).

As when you are affirming it means that the mind is permanently being purified, you should amplify the
30 affirmations as much as possible. For instance, it is excellent to take any texts from the Bible or passages from other scriptural writings that bear on the subject. While treating, care must be taken not to use passages in the Bible such as, " *A thousand shall fall at thy side . . . but it shall not come nigh thee* " (Ps. 91 : 7), or, " *Perfect love casteth out fear* " (1 John 4 : 18), as this is believing in the existence of the evil. They are correct statements with regard to the material so-called world, and may help a materially minded person, but not those who are relying
40 upon their realization of God for help. Such texts as, " *In thy presence is fulness of joy* " (Ps. 16 : 11), are excellent.

If Possible give only the Method and not Details.

In teaching people how to work, it does not do to show them too much. It is better to give them the main lines, and let them work things out for themselves.

We should leave others free to follow individual convictions upwards, and avoid the guilt of attempting to deprive "*the sons of God*" of their divine rights of freedom, and so unwittingly fight against God, and cloud the glorious view unfolding, which blesses each and all. Jesus said to inquisitive Peter : "*What is that to thee ?* 10 *follow thou me*" (John 21 : 22). We should mind our own business. We have quite enough to do to look after our own thoughts. If we are doing this well, we are doing very well.

The above method of working is only one amongst many. The principal thing is to stop blaspheming God, by thinking wrongly of His creation, and to get right away from all thought of the patient, his troubles, and the material world, keeping yourself actively thinking of God, or God's perfect world, and what takes place 20 there. This active, conscious communion with God is, "*Emmanuel, which being interpreted is, God with us*" (Matt. 1 : 23).

CHAPTER VI

SELFLESSNESS, TRUE LOVE, AND PURITY ESSENTIAL

Reverse Every Wrong Thought.

ISAIAH said : "*Let the wicked forsake his way ; and the unrighteous man his thoughts*" (ch. 55 : 7). We all want to do this. How are we to do it ? There is only 30 one scientific method. If a man is working properly, every time a wrong thought about any one else comes into his mind he has to reverse it ; that is to say, he has to get right away from all thoughts of the material person and think only of God and heaven, denying the existence of the evil in heaven, and realizing the perfection of the opposite good. If one does this properly, then the trouble instantly disappears. This is because the belief in the evil in your own subconscious mind is destroyed, and as there is only one subconscious mind, called the devil, the ether, mortal mind, etc., if you destroy the belief in your own subconscious mind, the evil is destroyed in the subconscious mind of the person in trouble, and measurably in that of everyone else.

For the first two years, working in this way, quite impersonally, I do not think I ever saw anything that was wrong in the street, such as men fighting, a man drunk or in an epileptic fit, or somebody crying, without
10 the trouble being instantly put right as I reversed the thought and got my thought clear. My first failure was the case of a bad epileptic fit at Westminster Bridge Underground Station, when I had only about five minutes to catch my last train at Waterloo. After this I had a percentage of failures until I had sufficiently advanced not to mind in the slightest what the result was. We have to reverse our thoughts because it is the right thing to do, and not to mind whether the demonstration takes place and the person is appreciably helped or
20 not. We must know the truth and refuse to give evil any power or even any place in our thoughts. What happens is not our business.

God Works, not Man.

In the course of treatment I realize for every patient that God works, not man ; and as this might tend to lower one's idea of man, in order to regain the sense of man's perfection I continue by realizing that man is divine, a perfect being in a perfect world, governed by a perfect God. The object of realizing that God works, not man,
30 is to get away from all sense of responsibility. We naturally cannot think we are doing anything ourselves, and what we have to recognize is that the result has absolutely nothing to do with us in any shape or way. It is simply due to the imaginary mist of matter thinning in front of the spiritual reality of the patient.

Be Loyal to God.

When you treat you should not treat to obtain results, as you then are believing in the evil. You should treat to be loyal to God, to give evil no power whatsoever in
40 your mind. You must not even be grateful for a demonstration, as this is blaspheming ; it is believing that " *God*

created man in his own image" and *"likeness"* (Gen.
1 : 26–27), and made him so badly that trouble took
place, and then you are grateful because God, having
made man badly, put him right. The only legitimate
thing to be grateful for is that God exists and that you
are part of His infinite consciousness, with all the benefits
arising therefrom. This is the teaching of the following
verse : *" Notwithstanding in this rejoice not, that the
spirits are subject unto you ; but rather rejoice, because
your names are written in heaven "* (Luke 10 : 20)   10

Selflessness Necessary.

In order to obtain really good results, we have to be
absolutely selfless, never caring in the slightest what is
going to happen. *" I do nothing of myself "* (John 8 : 28).
We must not rely on our own human opinions and try
to use our own human will. *" Be not conformed to this
world ; but be ye transformed by the renewing of your mind,
that ye may prove what is that good, and acceptable, and
perfect will of God "* (Rom. 12 : 2). We have to *" be
still, and know that I am God "* (Ps. 46 : 10). We have 20
to rely on God and allow the action of God to take place.
" The Father that dwelleth in me, he doeth the works "
(John 14 : 10). *" And greater works than these shall he
[that believeth on me] do "* (John 14 : 12). For we are
" workers together with him " (2 Cor. 6 : 1). *" We are
labourers together with God "* (1 Cor. 6 : 1). The action
of God—from a theological point of view—destroys the
evil thoughts that come and harm us, and if we will only
rely sufficiently upon God, and keep on praying in the
right method, ultimately all difficulties disappear. Even 30
fear becomes a thing of the past, *" For the Lord shall be
thy confidence "* (Prov. 3 : 26). We are so apt to try
and get our own will carried out, which is more like
teaching God His business than prayer, true prayer being
active, conscious communion with God, holy adoration.
We can rest on God. If you find that you cannot treat,
namely, actively think of God and heaven, then *" Rest
in the Lord, and wait patiently for him "* (Ps. 37 : 7),
" and he shall give thee the desires of thine heart " (ver. 4).
In other words, think quietly of some simple idea ; 40
think, for instance, of the peace or harmony in heaven,
and soon you will be treating, thought after thought of

that perfect world coming to you without any disturbing thought of the material world.

One result of this is a curious double mental outlook. On the one hand we have to have an intense desire to be of what use we can to the world. This is true love, and if we have not got it we have continually to work for it by the realization of God as Love, and man—spiritual man—as absolutely loving, until it comes. On the other hand, we must not care in the slightest what is going to 10 happen after we have treated. If we have an anxious feeling to help, then that means we are thinking of our patients as being ill or wanting help, and harm then follows. The spiritual man has the great desire to help, but does not trouble about what happens afterwards. He knows that all is perfect.

True Love Essential.

Love is the essence of all true work. I have never had a case where, if I have been truly loving towards patients, they have not been healed instantaneously. Sometimes 20 I have had to work for hours on end, once all through the night, before I could get a sense of love towards my patient. When I had obtained this, there was an instantaneous and wonderful result.

One of the difficulties in understanding the Bible is that it is sometimes impossible to give the niceties of the Greek words in the English language. One noticeable instance is that of the Lord's Prayer. Another is when, after dining by the lake of Tiberias, our Lord said to Peter : " *Simon, son of Jonas, lovest thou me more than* 30 *these ?* " Here the word translated " lovest " means the real spiritual love, the love of God. This is shown by the use of the Greek verb " *Agapao.*" Our Lord tried to lift Peter on to a spiritual basis, but Peter did not respond, as is shown in his reply, " *Yea, Lord ; thou knowest that I love thee.*" The Greek verb here used by Peter is *phileo*, which Robert Young, in his most useful analytical concordance, defines as " to be a friend." Our Lord a second time tried to lift Peter, but again Peter failed to grasp the spiritual idea. Our Lord then a third 40 time said, dropping to Peter's level, " *Lovest thou me ?* " Here he used the verb *phileo*, and Peter again responded, using the same verb *phileo* (John 21 : 13–17).

Human love is human affection, and is personal. Spiritual love is impersonal. It is the love of God, God's love, the spiritual man.

The Mark in the Forehead.

What is this love that we have to show towards our fellow-man ? It is your real self. It is the true spiritual love which comes shining through the mist of matter and gives the wonderful look on the face of one who truly loves with a pure holy love. When the mist thins sufficiently on successive pictures, it is seen as the marvellous look that appeared on the face of St. Stephen when he was stoned ; as the look which appeared on the face of Moses when he came down from the mountain ; and to a still greater degree it was seen on the face of our Lord on the Mount of Ascension. This look is seen in a lesser degree on the face of those who are referred to in Revelation 7 : 3, as *" the servants of our God,"* who are *" sealed in their foreheads."* In Revelation 14 : 1, they are spoken of as having *" his Father's name written in their foreheads."* Ezekiel 9 : 4 refers to it as *" a mark upon the foreheads of the men that sigh and that cry"* for the evil of the latter days. This is the soft bright look that appears in the eyes of those who know how to pray in the right way, *i.e.* by the realization of God and His manifestation. These are called in Revelation and elsewhere *" the elect,"* and are spoken of by St. Paul in Romans 11 : 5 as *" a remnant according to the election of grace."* *" Grace"* is the action of God which makes man pray. In Romans 9 : 27 he calls them *" a remnant," " of the children of Israel,"* which *" shall be saved,"* which shall have no punishment through their own wrong thinking as the troubles come on the world.

The Holy City.

It was the holy and blessed City, the love which one has to build in one's heart, which was described in the " new sayings of Jesus " from Oxyrhynchus, in the following words : " The kingdom of heaven is within you, and whoever shall know himself shall find it. Strive, therefore, to know yourselves, and ye shall be aware that ye are the sons of the Almighty Father, and ye shall know that ye are in the City of God, and ye are the City."

4

The love has to be so universal that even when you are
with a person and have an intense desire to help him, the
feeling must be to help humanity in general. To help an
individual we have to get away as much as we can from
any sense of personality. This is always more or less
troublesome. If your love is a true love, people feel it.
The mere fact of being in your presence makes them feel
happy and contented if you are thinking rightly. The
reason is, that when you are doing your work properly,
reversing any wrong thoughts that come into your so-
called mind, the evil thoughts attacking them get
destroyed, and only peaceful and happy thoughts can
come to them. The test as to whether your love is a true
love or only a personal attachment, and therefore an
hypnotic effect, is, I think, this : When you love being
with people and enjoy interchanging ideas with them,
this is quite right. Your intercourse with everyone
should be of this nature. If, however, you find that when
you are away you are constantly thinking of them and
wishing you were with them, then this is a sign that it is
not true love, but that there is an hypnotic action taking
place, and you have to be careful, and treat, steadily and
persistently, until this effect has all gone. Treat for love,
for purity, and against hypnotism. You do not improve
the position by running away from it ; you have to fight
it out. If by circling round the candle you would singe
your wings or put out the candle, naturally you have to
keep away and treat until the danger is done away with
by the treatment that has taken place. The mere turning
away from evil never destroys it. It has to be faced and
fought scientifically, and that always results in victory.

Purity is Essential.

When you are working for love you have continually
to work also for purity, until no love for another on your
part, however great, can raise any feeling of personality
in their mind whatsoever. If the personal feeling arises
it is not their fault, but your joint misfortune, because
it prevents the wonderful happiness and peace that comes
from the interchange of perfect, pure love. The greatest
happiness in the world is obtained from loving someone
intensely and being loved intensely in return. This true
happiness can only be gained by what is practically perfect

purity. This can be obtained by the constant realization of God as Spirit, the Principle of all purity and holiness. Then not only do you begin to understand in some degree what heaven and the love of God are like, but you begin to let other people have the same uplifted thoughts.

I suppose all pure-minded, loving people, and many who are not so fortunate, have felt, more or less, the intense yearning to have a pure and perfect love that is dependent upon no magnetic attraction and can be indulged in without any fear of evil resulting through lack of control. This can be obtained, but only by persistent daily, in some cases hourly, work, which will enable us to become as impersonal in our love as in our treatment. This constant prayer for purity, knowing that the action is taking place at the time when you are tempted, has to be carried out if you wish to heal instantaneously everybody who comes to you. It is my opinion, although it is not shared by some good workers, that our Lord never had to work for purity, as he was born of a virgin, and therefore the whole of his time could be given to other work that we wish to do—for instance, in becoming more selfless—but for which we have not time.

The Virgin Birth Scientific.

Now that we know what the facts of the world are, we know that the Virgin Birth is absolutely scientific, and came through the millions of workers of the Hebrew race who prayed for the forthcoming Messiah. This is why " *she was found with a child of the Holy Ghost* " and why " *the angel of the Lord*"—or uplifted thought—" *appeared unto Joseph,*" saying " *that which is conceived in her is of the Holy Ghost* " (Matt. 1 : 18–20). " *The Holy Ghost* " is the action of God on man which makes man pray ; it is also called " *grace* " in the Bible. The pictures constituting Joseph as a father disappeared with the prayers. This is why our Lord was of the lineage of Joseph just as much as we are of the lineage of our fathers. In our case the pictures were not improved in such a wonderful manner.

At one time, even when I had over twenty-five patients, for whom I was treating every day, I used to treat myself for love, purity, and wisdom between the treatment for each patient. In those days, although I

was excessively busy with my professional duties, I some-times had between twenty and thirty patients, for whom I treated daily, but instead of averaging ten to twenty minutes for each treatment, as I do now, my average was four or five minutes. This was because, instead of the major portion of the time being taken up with improving the patient mentally and morally, lifting him on to a more spiritual basis, so that he himself could heal sin and disease in the way that our Lord did, my time used to be
10 given chiefly to healing the physical troubles. A little time, perhaps a quarter of the total time, was given to helping the patients morally. To-day it is exactly the reverse; about three-quarters of the time is given to help-ing them mentally and morally. The result in the past of the physical help was not so very much inferior to what it is now; but I am at present disappointed if I cannot get a patient to start healing others of sin and disease and getting noticeable results within a few weeks' time.

Fortunately to get results a man has only to do his
20 best to think of God in the way pointed out, and not to think that the action of God is not going to take place. It is not upon the clearness of the realization, it is upon the degree to which we get away from all thoughts of the material world, that the healing depends. Whether we get it clear or not is measured, to human sense, by the amount of the evil that has to be destroyed.

Repetition is of Value.

It is necessary to use a certain amount of repetition in writing articles such as these on prayer, as, to be-
30 ginners, there is so much entirely new information ; so that, when one is making a certain point, it is necessary to repeat oneself often to enable the reader to under-stand that point properly.

When a thing is difficult to grasp, saying it over several times drives it well into the reader's mind. What happens when an intelligent man first reads a statement of Truth is that he grasps it intellectually. We have to go further than this, however. We have to grasp a thing so that it becomes ingrained in us, and, as Tolstoi puts it,
40 "it becomes of the heart." A new fact that has been grasped intellectually has to be driven home and made part of oneself, as it were. Then, when you are thinking

over other new statements of Truth, or the policy you
are going to adopt, this fact has become so fixed in your
mind that it is no longer necessary to think consciously
of it as a fact, whilst you are weighing the *pros* and *cons*
of what the new statement of Truth means, or what you
are going to do. This unconscious habit of mind only
comes about by constantly thinking of the new statement
of Truth as a fact, and this is achieved by constant
repetition of it in one form or another.

While it is not a good plan to give a person too many 10
details of how to pray, it is necessary to show the principles on which to work, and it is valuable to show details
of the actual method of working, so that people can
develop this true method of prayer in the way they find
suits them best. This is fully set out in a book called
*Treatment, or Healing by True Prayer.**

CHAPTER VII

SIGNS OF THE FINAL TROUBLES

Preliminary Signs of the Final Troubles.

SHORTLY before writing this, I had a letter from 20
Minnesota, in which the writer says : " I am of
opinion that all matter will be destroyed through ' fire,'
which I think is the only way a proper purification of all
into spirit can take place. Am I right ? "

The writer would be correct about matter being
destroyed by fire at the end of the world if there
were no such thing as true prayer. This destruction
by fire is shown in numerous places in the Bible,
almost all the prophetical books refer to it, and it is also
shown that by true prayer the horrors therefrom will be 30
reduced.

Jesus said : " *Except those days should be shortened,
there should no flesh be saved : but for the elect's sake those
days shall be shortened* " (Matt. 24 : 22). Isaiah 26 : 3
shows that those who know how to pray by the realization of God will have no trouble. He says : " *Thou wilt*

---

*Lists of books dealing with this subject are obtainable from the
Book Department of the Society for Spreading the Knowledge of
True Prayer, founded by F. L. Rawson. Present Address: 12 Bucking-
ham Palace Gardens, London, S.W. 1, England.

keep him in perfect peace, whose mind is stayed on thee."
Daniel shows this deliverance in chapter 12 : 1, and also
shows how God's people, those who understand how to
be in communion with God, will be delivered, namely,
by the denial. He has just concluded the prophecy
which shows the end of Napoleon (and, owing to history
repeating itself, of the ex-Kaiser of Germany) as follows :
" He shall come to his end, and none shall help him " ;
then he continues : *" And at that time shall Michael*
10 *stand up, the great prince which standeth for the children*
of thy people : and there shall be a time of trouble, such
as never was since there was a nation even to that same
time : and at that time thy people shall be delivered."
Michael is the denial of the existence of the evil in
heaven ; Gabriel is the affirmation or dwelling upon the
perfection of the opposite.

Since the 4th edition of *The Nature of True Prayer*,
I have started a monthly paper called *The Weekly*
Lessons and Bulletin,* in which I give, firstly, a state-
20 ment of the trouble attacking the world which requires
to be worked against by prayer. Secondly, a lesson for
senior students which at present consists of details of
the Bible prophecies of the troubles which are coming at
the end of the world, the fulfilment thereof, and the
scientific explanation of how they are coming about.
Thirdly, a graduated course of lessons for junior students,
commencing with ordinary psychology, and consisting
of twenty-four lessons extending over two years, at the
end of which time I will probably be giving them the
30 highest I am capable of giving.

I also give details of any troubles in our Centres
throughout the world which require to be overcome ; as
a rule, asking the workers in two adjacent towns to take
up and pray against the difficulties.

Evil cannot bring about Good.

Many think these troubles are turning men to God in
the way that the Great War is said by some to have done
in Europe. This is not correct, as evil cannot bring about

* The publication of *The Weekly Lessons and Bulletin* ceased in
40 March 1923. *Active Service*, the official organ of the movement, continues to be published by The Society for Spreading the Knowledge of
True Prayer, 12 Buckingham Palace Gardens, London, S.W.1, England.

good. As these troubles increase, so will men more and more turn in thought to God with increasing joy and thankfulness, finding this the only certain method of overcoming their difficulties. It is believed by many that evil is, therefore, a good thing because it turns men to God. This is not the case ; it is far better that a man should turn to God without having the evil. The nature of evil, however, is self-destructive ; evil always destroys itself if given time. Every form of sin ultimately so punishes the sinner that he gives it up. 10

Some thinkers say it is the false idea of pleasure through sin which tempts the sinner. This is not really so. It is the thoughts that act on a man, which cause him to sin. Thought after thought comes, giving the desire, and then at last, sad to say, strong enough thoughts come, which cause him to sin.

Sin gives no Pleasure.

When a man knows more, he finds that sin gives no pleasure whatsoever, and so he does his very best to give up sinning. All the happiness there is in sin he can 20 obtain without it. Sin only reduces the happiness. Pleasure comes through thoughts acting upon the mind right in this respect, and is irrespective of the sin. Sometimes thoughts of sin and of happiness come at the same time, sometimes they do not. In the cinematographic pictures (to which I have earlier compared material man and the material world), as far as I am aware, you never get sin without subsequent evil thoughts attacking the sinner, apparently due to the sin, but not really so ; for there is no cause and effect in the material world. The 30 evil which overtakes the wrongdoer is in the cinematographic pictures following after the sin. If there were cause and effect in the material world the sinner would be bound to get the punishment after the sin, but if a man treats he can overcome the punishment for his sin. Every time he overcomes the punishment he is less likely to sin in future. The difficulty is that the feeling of the justice of the punishment makes it difficult for him to treat and get right away from all thought of the material world, either past or present. If he could, the punish- 40 ment would cease, and ultimately the sin would cease.

One of the proofs of the above is that if a man is in

the habit of going to a public-house and obtaining pleasure from intoxication, and, seeing him about to enter, you treat so that the desire goes and he does not enter, you will find that he will lose none of the pleasure that he would have derived from the drinking. It is true that he will give you some material reason why he appeared to have had happiness; it may merely be from the feeling that he had been able to refrain from his vicious habit. You can destroy the evil, but you cannot
10 in any way destroy the good, and therefore whilst the desire for drink goes, the pleasure remains, the latter being caused by thoughts of happiness acting upon a mind that is fortunately in the condition to respond to them.

Sin always followed by Punishment.

Man ultimately finds that sin is always followed by punishment, and that the only way in which he can prevent this punishment is by true prayer. It is not right that a man should be punished when he sins, because he never made his so-called mind, and he never made the
20 thoughts that attack him. *" Behold I was shapen in iniquity; and in sin did my mother conceive me"* (Ps. 51 : 5). It is one of the many proofs that this material world is hell. At the same time the punishment appears to deter many from sinning, although, as a matter of fact, it does not.

Ignorance brings just as much punishment in many cases as sin does. The punishment is caused by evil thoughts attacking the mind, and when a man knows how to pray, he can destroy these evil thoughts and free himself
30 from the punishment. When he does this, he is less liable to trouble in the future, as his so-called mind is improved. Then neither the sinful thoughts nor the thoughts causing the punishment have quite the same effect.

One of the best realizations wherewith to avoid the punishment is that " it never happened, man is spiritual and divine." One should never allow oneself to dwell even for a moment on the occasion when the sinful thoughts overcame one. Remember it is not you who sin; it is merely the evil thoughts which play upon an
40 apparent you, that cause the effect of a man appearing to sin. By refusing to dwell upon the apparent sin, and dwelling instead upon the perfection of the world of

reality, you destroy the evil thoughts that tempt you, and, what is of more importance, gradually change your mind so that no sinful thoughts can touch you, and you are permanently free. Esdras pointed this out in his account of the end of the world. He wrote : " *Let not your sins weigh you down, and let not your iniquities lift up themselves : woe be unto them that are bound with their sins* " (2 Esdras 16 : 76–77).

Forgiveness of Sins.

When a man sins, it is not his fault, it is his mis-fortune ; and this is why we have not to punish the sinner. Sin metes out its own punishment, and if a man is doing evil, we have to forgive in the only true way, namely, by the destruction of the thoughts attacking him, and the purification of his mind. This we do by destroying all thoughts of the evil in our own mind, and knowing the allness of God, good. There is no sinner, only our false concept of God's man. If we reverse our thoughts properly, he will never sin again, and this is the only true forgiveness.

The witness who accepts the false evidence, and continues thinking that the man is sinning, is participating in the sin, and gets punished. " *Let none of you imagine evil in your hearts against his neighbour* " (Zech. 8 : 17). It is the business of those who know how to think rightly, to protect such a man from the consequences of the evil, as it is not, as has been said, his fault, but his misfortune. For as St. Paul says : " *Therefore thou art inexcusable, O man, whosoever thou art that judgest : for wherein thou judgest another, thou condemnest thyself* " (Rom. 2 : 1).

CHAPTER VIII

SPIRITUAL REALITIES OF THE BODY

Heaven a World of Four Dimensions.

SINCE I first set this out over twenty years ago, scientific men have come to the conclusion that there is a world of four dimensions of which we only see three.

Professor Einstein has stated that the fourth dimension is time, that is to say, there are four independent quantities, which locate an event. These are length,

breadth, thickness, and time. The difficulty in understanding the Einstein theory is that whilst mathematical
symbols enable one to express the properties conveyed by
these words, it is impossible to form any mental picture,
by words or otherwise, which accurately expresses them.

Ouspensky, the Russian engineer, says that we look
through a slit ; every moment the present becomes the
past, and the future becomes the present, but both are
there. He says that this past and future is the fourth
dimension, of which we only see the present world of three
dimensions, which latter is a purely illusionary world.

Heaven is a world of four dimensions, of which we see
only three, and therefore see it all falsely. If anything is
wrong in the material world, and we can turn in thought
to heaven and realize sufficiently clearly the spiritual
reality of what appears to be taking place in the material
world, the material world changes for the better. The
imaginary mist of matter thins and you see heaven a little
more as it really is ; a well man instead of a diseased one,
a happy man instead of a miserable one, a man with
plenty instead of a man who is hard up. When you are
praying, the more nearly that which you are thinking
about resembles what is really taking place in heaven, the
better the result you obtain. In this way we prove what
God and heaven are like. This does not mean that a
person could not get an equally good result without understanding what is taking place in heaven, but it needs a
much more spiritual and much clearer realization of God
to get a similar result when you are thinking of God alone,
than when you are thinking of the details of what is
taking place in heaven. The reason for this is that when
thinking of the details of what is happening in heaven,
it is much easier to get right away from the material
world and be thinking actively of the world of reality ;
also when you realize God alone, you are helping your
patient mentally and morally as well as physically, and
much more matter has to cease its imaginary existence.

It is better for people, if they can, to work out for
themselves the spiritual realities of the different things
they see about them ; but there is so little time now left
until the final end of all matter, and people are so very
ready for the truth and keen to put into practice what
they know, that there is not the same fear now of what

may be called mental indigestion as there was when I started over twenty years ago. Then one could not give a man much to think of, as he could not take it in ; it was so opposed to his old false ideas. Now the majority of people are reaching out for Truth, and it is therefore easier for them to grasp new ideas, and consequently for them to protect themselves from the troubles around, and the more serious ones which are coming and which they already begin to feel are " in the air." In other words, the mist is thinning all over the world and we are seeing men more as they really are—knowing instead of not knowing.

Everything has its Spiritual Reality.

Heaven being a world of four dimensions, of which we see only three, it is clear that everything about us has its spiritual reality. When you know what this is, and you turn and think of heaven *and* the spiritual realities, you get a much better idea of what heaven is like.*

The spiritual reality of the good which you see around you is the same description of good. For instance, when a man is loving towards you, the spiritual reality of that man is being loving towards your spiritual self. God is Love, and the only way in which God can show his love towards your real self is by the love that your fellow-man shows towards you. God works by means of the real man, man being God's consciousness. When your material self is loving to a person, it is really God loving, and it is the love of God, or your spiritual self, that is shining through your material self. The wonderful and beautiful look which we see on the face of a person who is loving with a pure and holy love, is the real man shining through the mist of matter. Unfortunately, on account of the mist of matter, we see the love very imperfectly ; in fact, often we do not see it at all.

So, when a man is angry, even angry with you, if you can realize the love that is really there all the time, although you may not be conscious of it, instantly the man stops being angry, and is loving. This applies not only to human beings, but to animals.

* These spiritual realities are defined in *Life Understood*, by F. L. Rawson, M.I.E.E., A.M.I.C.E., the standard work on Mental Healing (6th edition, 15s. ($5.00). Postage 1s.). Published by The Society

The Society for Spreading the Knowledge of True Prayer

14a, Eccleston Street, London, S.W.1, England.

The Spiritual Realities of a Human Being.

The next thing of importance to understand is the spiritual reality of a human being. Man specifically, means all the spiritual beings in heaven, which Paul speaks of as the Christ. This is God's consciousness, which is as infinite as God. Everywhere where God is, man is. Man is the activity or thinking of God, God's thinking. Paul said, "*Christ the power of God, and the wisdom of God*" (1 Cor. 1 : 24).

10 At one time I was treating to know what Paul meant when he spoke of "*the Christ*," and what was meant by "*the rod of iron*" referred to in Rev. 2 : 27. I was suddenly called at a moment's notice over to France to treat for a man who was out of his mind. The following morning I was sitting on his bed by his side, and he was in one of his raving fits. I was afraid lest at any moment he would spring at me, and kept my hand close to my neck so that he should not catch hold of my throat. At the same time I knew that my only safety was to keep my 20 thought fixed steadily on the world of reality. I knew that if I allowed myself to think of the man as springing at me he would be at me at once. I was therefore realizing, as clearly as I could, the real man, God's man—the actual words I was using were : "Man is spiritual, perfect, divine"—getting clearer and clearer as I made my statements, mentally gripping the position, the fact of being, so to speak, when suddenly the thought came : "It is the power of God," and my hand fell down by my side, and the man was perfectly natural and quiet. His 30 words were : "What a lovely day it is!" At once it flashed into my mind that this realization was "*the rod of iron*," that is, the mental grip which was almost like a mental vice, which held the spiritual idea and prevented any thought of the material coming into the mind.

The Christ the "Power of God."

I also saw at once the meaning St. Paul attached to "*the Christ*," because, as above quoted, he said that "*Christ*" is "*the power of God, and the wisdom of God.*" I had proved by an instantaneous result that man was 40 "*the power of God*" and that by "*the Christ*" St. Paul meant all the spiritual beings in heaven. I know now that this was his meaning, as shown by many passages in the Bible. When one proves the statements of fact by instantaneous results, the result must come, as you are thinking the thought. If you give a long treatment and heal a man instantaneously, putting in a new statement of fact, it is no proof that this new statement of fact is true, because he might have been healed during any portion of the treatment. For instance, on the day following the healing above mentioned, a lady asked for help, saying that her head was paining and troubling her. I commenced treatment audibly by stating : 10 " There is no mortal mind, there is only one Mind——" As I said this, she threw up both hands, crying, " I am well ! I am well ! " This is proof that there is only one Mind. That Mind is God.

In treating, when thinking of man, never think of an individual man if you can avoid it ; think of God's infinite consciousness. In fact, try always to get that sense of infinity when you are thinking of reality. Think of infinite Love, infinite Life, infinite Truth, infinite wisdom, etc.   20

When we come to consider man in detail, we find three different portions—the head, the body, and the limbs. When I was first retained by one of the leading London daily newspapers to make an examination for them into mental healing—an investigation which led me to devote my life to this work—I found that I had to turn all my old ideas topsy-turvy ; not a single one of them was correct. For instance, I used to think that man saw with his eyes, and heard with his ears, and I could talk learnedly to you about the different class of vibrations, 30 etc. Now I know that a man does not hear with his ears, or see with his eyes. From a natural science point of view, vibrations are transmitted along the lines of force of which the ether is composed, direct to the human mind, and sight and hearing are entirely mental effects. It would take too long to give the proof of this, but I might mention two facts.

Sight is Mental.

I once went with one of the best-known doctors to test another doctor, who found that he had intuitional 40 powers ; that is to say, his powers of sight were more developed than ours. By treatment I enabled him to see the sister of the first doctor lecturing 200 miles away, and out of about forty things he saw, which we noted in writing, there were only two unimportant items in which we found he was mistaken.

Hearing is Mental.

On another occasion a man came to consult me about his wife, who was speaking to her sister every day in America. He did not know what to do. He told me that he had tested it in every shape and way, and there 10 was no question about it, and he wished to know whether it was safe. I said, no. I was too full of work then to teach them how to develop their faculties by true prayer.

Recently a man wrote to me about his special powers of hearing the radio sounds. He had heard an opera which lasted for over two hours, and said that he could hear every note, although he found out afterwards it was being performed in a town several hundred miles distant. In Chicago some medical men have been testing a man who has this delicate sense of hearing, and say that he 20 has a radio ear. We all have radio ears but we do not know it.

I have given above the natural science view. As a matter of fact, there are no vibrations coming from the thing seen to the person seeing, nor from the person speaking to the person hearing. Everything, from a metaphysical point of view, is simply vibrations or thoughts passing to the human mind. When, for instance, a person appears to be telling you lies, it is simply you who are falsely thinking that there is a person there 30 who is lying to you. And so with everything else. All that we have to deal with is our own wrong thoughts about everything we see or hear.

The Capacity to Know God.

The same remark applies to every portion of the head ; the organs are not used. I was amazed one day, on finding out what the spiritual realities of the different portions of the head were, to discover that they exactly agreed with the position with regard to the material head, namely, the spiritual realities of the parts of the head 40 are not used in the actual doing of things in heaven. They are the capacity to do this, that, or the other. The eyes are the capacity to discern ; the ears the capacity to understand ; the nose the capacity to pursue a train of thought ; the teeth the capacity to analyse and dissect God's ideas. The head itself is the capacity to know God.

After I had found this out, I was interested to find that it was confirmed in the Bible. I was once asked to explain the eleventh chapter of 1 Corinthians. Treating for knowledge, I explained that it had to be taken spiritually, and amongst other things I stated, that when Paul said in the third verse, " *the head of every man is Christ*," he meant that Christ is man's capacity to know God. I ought to have added, " *and his manifestation*." There is only one Christ, and everyone has that Christ capacity to know any idea of God that may be needed.

The Body the Power of Doing Things.

The parts of the body are the actual power of doing these things. For instance, the hand is the power with which man grasps God's ideas ; the foot the power of concentration on these ideas ; the leg the power of movement from idea to idea.

I feel sure that the head has exactly the same number of parts in it as the body, as everything that a man does, he must naturally have the capacity to do.

Man made in the Image and Likeness of God.

When you come to consider the spiritual realities of the different parts of the body, it will help you when you recognize that the spiritual man is made in the image and likeness of God. Therefore, if you consider what God is, you will find that every aspect of God is represented in the spiritual man ; as God is Life, man has Life eternal, for God is his Life.

These, of course, have to be seen misrepresented in the material man, and you will find that this is so. For instance, there are three main views of God—Life, Truth, and Love. So there are three main organs in the material man. The lungs are the reflection or thinking of God as Life, the liver the reflection of God as Truth, and the heart the reflection of God as Love. This is why the heart has always been looked upon as having to do with love. Life brings you the ideas, Truth enables you mentally to digest and understand them, Love causes you to pass them on to your fellow-man to give him the happiness which you have received therefrom.

If we consider the other different views of God you will find that the so-called human mind is the reflection of God as Mind which gives the mental activities; the abdomen is the reflection of God as Soul which gives all wisdom and knowledge ; the kidneys as Spirit which gives all goodness and holiness ; the stomach as intelligence ; 10 the bones as substance which gives all permanence. The lymph is the reflection of God as Principle, the Principle of all peace, joy, energy, activity, law, and order, etc.

Man the Compound Idea of God.

Man, the real man in heaven, consists of an infinite number of ideas, and fresh ideas are continually coming to him as combinations of ideas. Each individual man consists of the combinations of ideas which have come to him, plus his Christ-consciousness, his capacity to know 20 any idea of God. Man never loses or forgets any idea that comes to him, because these ideas have become part of him, part of what St. Paul calls his spiritual or glorious body. It will be seen, therefore, that man's knowledge of God is always increasing, for the reason that the combinations of ideas coming to him are always increasing in number. As the number of God's ideas is infinite, the possible combinations are infinite. For this reason, this unfolding of the perfection of heaven continues for ever.

The material man needs to become as much like his 30 spiritual self as possible. He needs, therefore, to be mentally intensely active. Treatment, or true prayer, therefore, is not merely losing oneself in a sort of vague realization of Deity, but is intense mental activity, the continuous evolution of fresh ideas of God and heaven. It is advisable to obtain as good a knowledge as possible of what actually is taking place in heaven ; as then, in treating, your mind is full of your conception of what is taking place in heaven, and it is easy to detach yourself entirely from the material world and from thoughts of 40 matter, and to lose yourself in conscious communion with God, this being the end to be aimed at: We have to keep our gaze fixed on " *the things which are not seen : for the*

*things which are seen are temporal ; but the things which
are not seen are eternal* " (2 Cor. 4 : 18). This is St.
Paul's statement that the material world is not real, for
it is known scientifically that anything that is temporal,
namely, ever ceases to exist, is not real now, whatever it
may appear to be.

Spiritual Realities of the Parts of the Body.

Heaven being a world of four dimensions, of which we
see only three, everything about us has its spiritual
reality. St. Paul says : " *For the invisible things of him
from the creation of the world are clearly seen, being understood by the things that are made* " (Rom. 1 : 20). Many of
the great thinkers have taught this. In treatment, after
denying the principal troubles, I realize as clearly as I can
the spiritual reality of the part affected. Supposing, for
instance, a man has a wounded arm, with septic poison-
ing, I realize man's arm was never wounded, for man's
arm is the power with which he passes on God's ideas
to his fellow-man. That power is God's power, and
therefore could never be wounded ; it is spiritual and
perfect. The blood never can be poisoned ; it is the joy
that circulates right throughout man's consciousness,
and is pure and perfect.

After finding the spiritual reality of the part affected,
and realizing its perfection, it is a good plan to think of
any text or good quotation dealing scientifically with the
point at issue. Supposing, for instance, someone has lost
a dear one, and you were working to destroy the anguish,
you would realize that there is no misery, and then think
of the absolute joy and happiness in heaven. Afterwards
you could continue by realizing that " *all the sons of God
shouted for joy* " (Job 38 : 7), and end by realizing that
" *in thy presence is fulness of joy* " (Ps. 16 : 11).

How to prove the Truth of One's Ideas.

The only way of proving the truth of the above is by
results. The only spiritual reality which I had any
difficulty in finding out was that of the shoulder. Mrs.
Rawson and I one morning looked up all the references
to the shoulder in the Bible, and came to the conclusion
that the shoulder is God's support which enables one to
use one's arm, the arm being the power with which one

passes on the ideas of God to one's fellow-man to give him happiness therefrom.

As has practically always been the case, within forty-eight hours I had a chance of testing this. I was at one of the Christian Science testimony meetings, when a lady I knew came up and asked me whether I could give her any suggestions that would help her to treat for her shoulder. She had injured it some two years before, and told me that although three or four practitioners had at different times worked for her, besides working hard herself, she was no better. I had a talk with her, which ended with the words, " Your shoulder never was injured ; it is God's loving support." Some time afterwards I met her, and she told me the healing had been instantaneous, and she had had no return of any kind.

It is the instantaneous, permanent healing that shows whether one is working in the right way or not. At the same time, you must not forget that by strong hypnotic thinking you can apparently heal a man instantaneously, but if you watch the case carefully you will find that about three months afterwards trouble always arises, sometimes the same disease, sometimes another disease, and sometimes even a form of sin.

Man's Work in the Kingdom of Heaven.

To give an idea of how one finds out what the details of heaven are, I may mention that a business client once came to me for advice. He and his partner were the heads of an important firm of art engravers. He told me business was so slack that they were losing money steadily. They could go on for twelve months on credit, but they would be trading with other people's money, as their own capital was lost, and they did not know whether it would be right to do this. They had no work for their best seven men that week, but they were obliged to keep them, because if the men left, they would not be able to get good men of the kind when work came in. I had had a talk with him in the past about Right Thinking, and he had since obtained some wonderful results ; this made me ask him whether he had spoken to his partner on the subject. He said he had, but his partner was full of old theology and would not listen to any new ideas. However, I asked them to come and discuss their position, and invited them to lunch with me, knowing that if I spoke about spiritual matters in business hours the partner would probably think me mad.

At lunch the right moment to speak occurred, and at the end of an hour and a quarter he said, " I see the whole thing ; it is absolutely true." I then explained to him how one thought out matters and then put them to the test to see if they were true or not. I told him I did not know what was man's work in heaven, but if I did, and could get my realization clear, they would at once be out of their difficulties. I told him it must be something loving, because God is Love, and man is always loving towards his fellow-man. I also said that loving is helping one's fellow-man, but I could not, however, see how one man could help another man in heaven, since everything is done by God. Then I expect I treated, because my next words to him were : " The only thing I know of that takes place in heaven is that a constant succession of ideas comes to man. Man's work may be passing on these ideas to his fellow-man to give him the joy which he received when he had the ideas passed to him. We shall know in a day or two if this is true, because if it is, you will be out of your difficulties. If not, I shall have to think out something else, and try that." This was on Saturday, and on Tuesday I got a letter from the partner I knew best, full of thanks, and winding up by saying, " What has happened can best be expressed by the words of my partner, who has been at the works all day, and has just said to me, ' If this goes on we shall make a small fortune in no time.' Orders have poured in at the works and at the office all day, and we are full up with work for a long time to come."

The Spiritual Reality of Breathing.

Then I knew that man's work in heaven is the receiving of God's ideas and re-presenting, passing them on to his fellow-man. This may be more accurately spoken of as calling the attention of one's fellow-man to them. In the physical man this, in its simplest form, appears as breathing. Consequently in cases where there is a difficulty in breathing, one realizes that man is always receiving and re-presenting God's ideas. The throat is the channel in consciousness through which these ideas come and go ; and therefore in all diseases of the throat one should take it up in the way mentioned.

The Spiritual Reality of Eating.

Whilst on this subject, let me say that man's work is not confined merely to receiving ideas and passing them on. Sometimes man takes the combinations of ideas which come, and breaks them up and forms new combinations of ideas, also passing them on. In this way they radiate out in infinite Mind, giving infinite beings
10 joy and happiness. This, in its simplest form, in the material man appears as eating. Consequently in all difficulties of the internal organs that have to do with the digestion of food, one works on this basis.

CHAPTER IX

HOW TO HELP BEGINNERS

THE method which I have been in the habit of following is to get a beginner to write out the way in which he treats, dividing the treatment into two portions. The first is the portion of the treatment that is applicable
20 to every patient ; the second the portion that is applicable only to the troubles of the particular patient in question. Each denial should commence a new paragraph, and a space of about three-quarters of an inch should be left between each line. I shall be only too glad to help any reader if he will write out how he treats, and send it to me at my office in London, No charge is ever made for helping people to know how to treat.*

On receipt of this statement I write drawing attention to anything that may be wrong, and making suggestions.
30 I also ask him to try and amplify the affirmations he has written out. After he has been working in this way for about a week I ask him to correct it in accordance with my letter, and return it to me, when I again correct it.

* The Society for Spreading the Knowledge of True Prayer, founded by F. L. Rawson, is still carrying on this work. Written out treatments can therefore be sent to the Correspondence Department

The Society for Spreading the Knowledge of True Prayer

14a, Eccleston Street, London, S.W.1, England.

When it has been sent to me a second time, I again return it with any necessary alterations and suggestions, and suggest that he should work against some more of the universal evils, such as aggressive mental suggestion, and animal magnetism. In this way the use of formulæ, that is, groups of words which convey no adequate meaning to the person using them, is avoided. It would be easy to write out for anyone the method in which to treat, but this would be a formula, and most of the time of the patient would be taken up by trying to think what was meant, 10 instead of getting into conscious communion with God, and getting right away from all thoughts of the material world, as is the case when the person treating uses words the meaning of which he understands and appreciates.

The Lord's Prayer.

It is very difficult to draw a line exactly between what is a formula and what is not a formula. The Lord's Prayer, for instance, is a formula to anyone who knows nothing of religion, and yet, even in the form in which it is set out in the authorized version, it has helped 20 millions. People often quote it as showing that our Lord used supplicatory prayer. The difficulties in knowing what our Lord really said are many. For instance, the authorized version does not correctly translate the original Greek, because it is impossible to give the exact meaning in the English language. The old version, having been made from a Latin translation, could not in any case give the actual meaning the Saviour has given in the gospels ; Matthew and Luke use the Imperative Passive Mood, and the Latin has no Aorist. As Ferrar 30 Fenton says in his translation of the Bible, the force of the Imperative 1st Aorist seems to him to be that of what is called a " Standing Order," a thing to be done absolutely and continuously. The translation that Ferrar Fenton gives is as follows :

" Our Father in the Heavens ; Your Name must be being Hallowed ; Your Kingdom must be being restored. Your Will be being done both in Heaven and upon the Earth."

We do not even know if the Greek words accurately 40 express the meaning of our Lord, who, it is believed, spoke in the Aramaic tongue. In the Aramaic version

there is no future tense used. Even if the words more
or less expressed what he really said, we must remember
that Jesus was unquestionably speaking to people who
were on a purely material basis. Few have recognized
how terribly material the world was at that time. Those
who repeated his words were probably also on a material
basis, since even his disciples lacked true spiritual discernment until after he had made his final unparalleled
demonstration and emerged from the tomb. Even after
that, Peter completely misunderstood his teachings, as is
shown in Acts 5 : 8–10. Jesus had the whole world
against him. Unlike Mahomet, who fell on to a material
basis, he held the spiritual idea always aloft. When we
come to work in the way that Jesus taught, and strive
to follow in his footsteps, our admiration, veneration,
and gratitude for what he did becomes inexpressible, and
our wonder at his marvellous life-work deepens into
humble adoration, stirring our hearts to more earnest
desire to keep his commandments, as the only worthy
proof of our love.

Three Simple Rules.

Fortunately true prayer has nothing to do with any
theory, dogma, or creed ; it is simply a question of what
the Bible calls righteousness, namely, Right Thinking.
The whole basis of prayer is simply thinking of absolute
good, the highest good that you can possibly imagine ;
and whether you are an Atheist or an Agnostic, High
Churchman or Low Churchman, a Roman Catholic or a
Quaker, you will equally get your results if you will put
into practice the following three simple rules :

You must not Think of the Material World.

(1) In prayer, you must not think of the material
world or the person for whom you are praying at all.
" *Go not after other gods to serve them* " (Jer. 26 : 6).
All that is permissible is, when you start, to recognize
whom it is you desire to help. The results are in accordance with our intentions.

Only your Best Concept of Reality Necessary.

(2) You must form your very best concept of God and
of heaven and dwell upon it. " *Thou wilt keep him in
perfect peace whose mind is stayed on thee* " (Isa. 26 : 3).

The results are dependent, not upon the concept you may form ; they are dependent upon the degree in which you get away from all thoughts of the material world. This is the essence of true prayer. It can be spoken of as the thinning of the imaginary mist of matter which hides heaven from us, allowing God's world to be better seen. This is why you cannot be a fine healer unless you have an intense desire to help. This comes from the love you have, not " of " but " towards " your fellow-man. It is the love at the back of the work that makes you try to 10 form your very best concept of God and of heaven. This is why beginners often obtain marvellous results. Sometimes the results will be obtained through the realization of the real, spiritual man, sometimes as in my own case when I started, the results will come from simply turning in thought to God and heaven and realizing the infinite Love of that perfect world, the Love which is God.

Universal Love Necessary.

Personal love makes it more difficult to help. It is so difficult to prevent thinking of the loved one as wanting 20 help. You must keep your thoughts off them, to do the best for them. This is why St. Paul said : " *Henceforth know we no man after the flesh* " (2 Cor. 5 : 16).

It is not the personal love of one individual, but the love that comes welling from the heart towards everyone with whom you come in contact, that is necessary. This love loses nothing by being universal. It gains. Constant practice always improves, and the love for the individual grows as the love of humanity increases. You must not reduce the love for the most loved one. This must 30 steadily increase. But the love for the man in the street has to increase faster than the love for the most loved one, until the two are level, one helping the other upwards. Higher, still higher ! Then you begin to find what heaven is like. Each one you come in contact with adds to your joy, the pure, perfect joy of true love.

" Have Faith in God."

(3) " *Fear thou not . . . the Lord thy God in the midst of thee is mighty ; he will save* " (Zeph. 3 : 16, 17). You must not think that the action of God will not take 40 place, that God will not be God. This is where the mis-

taken belief in blind faith has started. You must not
think that what you want is going to happen. Any result
from this is purely hypnotic. By believing that a certain
thing you desire is going to happen you may even stop
your demonstration. The thing you desire may be harmful, and with your treatment the thoughts you are intensi-
fying may actually have to be destroyed before the proper
result can be arrived at and you are out of your trouble.

You have to possess what is signified by the Greek
10 word "*pistis*," which means " faith founded upon knowledge." In my own case it means that when I start to
help anyone I know to an absolute certainty that they are
going to be helped more or less ; because I know the
Principle that is at work. Also I know absolutely that
it is impossible for anyone to turn in thought to God and
heaven, with the object of helping someone, however
much of a beginner he may be, without that person being
helped more or less. In the ordinary cases I am certain
they are going to be healed quickly. I do not, however,
20 allow myself to think this for one moment. I would have
to reverse it at once. It would be blaspheming God,
thinking that God's world, the only world there is, was
imperfect, thinking that I had to help God to put His
world right.

At the same time I know full well, however, that I
have not sufficient faith, because I think that I am not
good enough, that is to say, have not yet sufficiently improved my so-called mind, that everything which comes
before me is instantaneously healed. This is the only
30 thing which stops the healing taking place. Improvement
is simply a question of doing sufficient treatment to get
the human mind sufficiently purified, so as to get rid of
any belief in a material person. You may say to me,
" Then why don't you do this, why don't you treat all
day long until your mind is in such a condition that everyone is healed instantaneously ? " I wish I could, but I
am not far enough on. A man cannot possibly do any
good of any kind or description except by turning in
thought to God, and it is only the action of God, called
40 "*the Holy Ghost*" or "*grace*," which causes this to take
place. Our Lord pointed this out some half a dozen
times. For instance : "*No man can come to me, except
the Father which hath sent me draw him*" (John 6 : 44).

Trying to do Things Materially is Useless.

All doing of material things is absolutely useless. It is simply part of the cinema pictures. You may retort : " But you write for *Active Service* ; you give audible treatments every morning and answer the questions of those present ; you have a large staff who are continually answering letters and healing sin and disease and devoting all their time to helping other people. You superintend all this." Yes, but it is because I am not far enough on to do something better. If I could sit down and give 10 twenty hours a day to treatment only, instead of helping people also in other ways, I should shortly be able habitually to heal everyone instantaneously who came. The effect of this on the world would be far greater than a dozen *Active Services* and several thousand assistants taking cases, and treating audibly and answering questions all day long, because it is the practical results which prove a man's theology. If one could heal everything instantaneously, and do this in the way I have pointed out, namely, by simply thinking of God and making 20 audible statements of Truth, one would prove the facts of the world, and practically every spiritually-minded clergyman and doctor in England would start to pray in this way, and the millennium would be upon us almost immediately. The regular instantaneous healing of bad troubles is one of the things that is going to happen shortly before the end of the world, and this is one of the things that will make almost every intelligent and loving man and woman turn in thought to God with the object of helping humanity. 30

Miraculous Results Obtainable.

If you will follow the above three rules implicitly, you will get marvellous results straight away. In one case a Roman Catholic came to me, owing to a friend, a dispensing chemist, having been helped. She thought she would like to be able to heal others in the same way. I did not deal with her theological beliefs. These were to be settled between her and her priest, but I showed her how our Lord prayed. Like a wise woman, she tested the information given by treating for the three worst 40 cases of which she knew. The first was an epileptic boy who, for some time, had been having half a dozen epileptic fits a day. He never had another. The other two were men who had been in lunatic asylums for some time. In one case the man was well in about a week, and in the other case it took a little longer.

Some months afterwards she told me that they had not let one of these cases out, as they thought it impossible that he could be well. I told her she should take this up and realize that " mortal mind could not possibly
10 keep man out of his place, because man is always in his right place, in Mind, in God, being part of God's consciousness by means of which God thinks and acts." The result of this was that instructions were received from Headquarters that they were to send home every patient the local authorities in the hospital thought could possibly be allowed to go home. So what benefited one benefited many, and about fifty were released.

CHAPTER X

MANIA AND DRINK

20 **Mania not Difficult.**

MANIA, as a rule, is not a difficult thing to heal. Sometimes, of course, one gets a difficult case. One of the best known men in England telephoned through one day to ask whether anything could be done for his private secretary, who for six months had been going out of her mind, and now would have to be put away. I asked him to send her to me. The day following her visit she wrote me a letter of thanks, saying that she had left behind in my room " the thing that had been
30 thinking, thinking, thinking." About a fortnight after, when she was with me learning more of Truth, a solicitor called for help. His brother had been in a lunatic asylum for two or three years, and he wanted to know whether he could be helped. All three of us went out to tea together, and at tea I told him that I was too full of patients to take his brother myself, and turning to the recently-healed patient, who was a bright, clever girl, I said, " You take him as a patient and help him." " Impossible," she said. " Why, I know nothing. It is quite impossible."
40 " You have not to do anything. It is God who does the

work," was my reply. " Ask her," and I turned to the solicitor. This he did, saying, " I am sure that you can help him." Thus pressed, she said she would try.

About four months afterwards a solicitor called upon me for technical advice about a new steel process that was being tested by the Admiralty. When we had finished, he said, " I do not think you recollect me, Mr. Rawson." " I am afraid that I do not." " Do you recollect at the beginning of the year I called to ask you whether you could help a brother of mine who was out of his mind ? You could not take him yourself, but whilst at tea you asked a young lady who herself had been healed, whether she would help my brother. Yesterday he came home absolutely well. Almost directly the treatment started, my brother commenced to improve. Within a month he appeared to be well, and the doctors allowed him to go for walks in the country with an attendant. In another month he was allowed to go out by himself, and within three months from the time treatment started, they said he was absolutely well and could return home directly the necessary formalities were completed." A few months after that, he was happily married, and, as far as I know, has been well ever since.

A few days later, I happened to mention this to a client of mine, who then said, " Do you remember, when first you told me about this, I asked you whether a person in an asylum could be helped, and you kindly showed me how to work ? I started that day, and in a week's time the person I was helping was out of the asylum. That person was my father, so you see I also have proved it to be true." This client, who is a clever engineer, has since had some wonderful results, and now recognizes and uses treatment as the only method whereby he can make a certainty of overcoming his various difficulties.

The Importance of Thinking only of Heaven.

These cases will show that it is not a question of what you think, but of how you think ; that it is the getting away from all thought of the material world, and not the concept you form of God, that is of importance.

At the same time it makes it easier if, instead of just trying to realize God, you try to realize what it is like in the real world, heaven, in respect of the troubles you apparently see in the material. In the case of mania, therefore, besides giving a general treatment, I realize that " man is never out of his mind, for Mind is God and man is always in Mind, in God, being God's consciousness, as infinite as God, reflecting divine wisdom, intelligence, and knowledge."

In addition, you want to work against all the details of the mania. Supposing, for instance, a man thinks that he is the King of England, I realize that " man never 10 thinks that he is the King of England because man knows Truth." Then again, if there is suicidal mania, I realize that " man can never want to kill himself, for man is in Mind, in God ; man's Life is God and man loves that Life." And so one takes every trouble, one after the other, denying their reality and affirming the perfection of the opposite. This is what Jesus meant when he said, " *If any man will come after me, let him deny himself, and take up his cross daily, and follow me* " (Luke 9 : 23). Deny that you are material, take up your difficulties 20 daily, and follow him in thought to God.

Drink.

One of the commonest forms of mania is what may be spoken of as the drink mania, because in most cases it is nothing more or less than diabolical possession, the devils being the tempting thoughts that come to make a man fly to alcohol in some form or other. There have been many cases of healing by true prayer, the large majority of which have been permanent.

In my own experience, until I went to America, where 30 I was unable to follow the cases, every case yielded with the first treatment, and I have only had one case where there has been any return. In that case, six months afterwards, the patient came to me with beads of perspiration standing out upon a deadly white face. In ten minutes after treatment had started, his appearance was normal, and shortly afterwards he left, completely recovered. He had been tempted to take a glass of wine two days previously, and had succumbed. Six months afterwards he came again for help, but in this instance 40 he had been able to come to me the following day. Nine months after this he had his last attack.

I had got in touch with him by meeting a man in the

train who told me of him, and said that his was one of the worst possible cases. Everything had been done for him by his friends, but without the slightest success, and several years before, one by one they had all given him up. I told him to send him to me when he could find him, and not to say why he was to come, but merely to say that I would be able to help him. He turned up on a Monday, and we had a talk, when he told me his miserable story and asked for help, which I said I would give him. On the following day he said, " On what day did you first treat for me ? " I replied, " Yesterday I started to treat regularly, but you got your first treatment on Friday when I received the letter about you, because, on reading it, I had to turn the ugly picture out of my mind and realize what God's man is." " That is extraordinary," he said, " because on Friday all wish for drink passed right out of my life." As mentioned above, this turned out not to be the case ; the reason being that he never would learn how to pray for himself, or take any trouble ; such was the condition of his mind, and consequently the work had to be done for him.

Three or four years ago I had to attend a meeting to advise some clients who were making a large contract for the supply of goods. Afterwards one of the principal men came up to me and said, " You do not recognize me." He turned out to be the quondam drunkard. He had married a charming wife, had several children, was the London head of an important business, and had never had any trouble from his old enemy. When he first came to me, which was about seventeen or eighteen years ago, he had on a straw hat, a disreputable frockcoat, a pair of trousers that were, if possible, worse, and boots open to the air. These were the sum-total of his worldly possessions.

My First Case of Drink.

The first case I ever had was that of a man well known in the literary world, who used to live near me. Several times a week he would come home by the last train, hardly able to get into a cab. I had tried to get him to have help from a practitioner, but he would not. He was a Roman Catholic, and said that it was his own fault. If he would only act on the advice of his priest he would

be all right, but he did not do so. One night, going home, when he was sober, I said to him, " I am only a beginner (I had known of Science for a month or two) but would you like me to try and help you ? " He gripped my shoulder like a vice, and said, " If you knew what a hell upon earth it is for me, you would do anything you could to save me." The last time I saw him was eighteen months after, when he told me that he had never had any trouble from that day. He sometimes drank a
10 glass of wine, but he never had any desire to take it— all wish for stimulants had gone.

In this case I took as my leading thought, " man cannot possibly touch such a beastly, filthy thing as drink, for man is spiritual and divine." It is not a very refined way of putting it, but results are what one desires, and in a matter of this kind, where it is all experimental tuition, I do not change my method of treatment as long as I find it thoroughly effective. I usually continue, " Man has no desires, man has everything he needs ; God's
20 ideas continually unfold to man, idea after idea, and only God's perfect, pure, and holy ideas can come to man."

My Second Case of Drink.

My second case of the cure of drink mania was an interesting one. A man wrote to the *Daily Express* asking if there was any cure for spinal sclerosis, and they sent him on to me. The following day a man who had come with him, called to see me, and said, " I could not speak to you yesterday because of that gentleman with
30 me. Is there any hope for me ? I have been a confirmed drunkard for many years. I have tried every possible cure in England and in America, and have absolutely failed to find any relief." And this in spite of the fact that he was a most religious man. Some months after, when he gave his first public testimony at a Testimony Meeting at which I was present, he said that he had drunk all his money away, then he had drunk his business away, then his friends, and then his relations, and, finally, had drunk away his wife and children. Ultimately he had
40 found himself in America absolutely penniless, glad to pick up any food he found in the streets. Now life was a continual source of happiness to him. He had never had

a temptation to drink since the day I first presented the truth to him.

I had not seen or heard anything of him for many years, when a few months ago he called to see me. He looked the picture of health, and told me that he had a fruit farm, and was doing very well; he had sold, I think, 80 tons of fruit the previous year. He was up, he said, every morning at four o'clock, and did as good a day's work as any man on the farm, although he was over seventy years of age.   10

The Reward of Trust in God.

I asked whether he still treated every day, and he told me that he had never gone back, but the best answer would be to tell me what had happened a week or so before. His daughter had run a crochet needle with a large hook deep into her hand. They would not send for a doctor, but relied upon treatment. Although there was no festering, the hook still remained in place, and treatment seemed to have no effect. A couple of days later, while passing the doctor's house in the morning, he 20 felt that he must go in and tell him to come and cut the hook out, it was such a simple way out of their difficulty. Just as he was going in at the gate it came to him that for nearly fifteen years he had relied upon God to get him out of every difficulty, and had always found the help he needed, why should he go back now? He at once turned towards home treating as clearly as possible. On arriving at his house, his daughter rushed to him holding up the crochet needle, saying that about five or ten minutes before, it had suddenly come out without any 30 pain or trouble. She showed him her hand, and there was hardly a mark to show where the needle had come out. Probably when treating previously, they had always unconsciously had the thought that perhaps the easiest plan would be simply to have the hand lanced, and this had prevented them from really getting their thought clear.

Remember that the whole point lies in getting away from the thought of the material world and losing yourself in conscious communion with God. If you have at 40 the back of the mind a lurking desire to go to a doctor or to take drugs or use other material remedies, it makes

it more difficult for you. This is why so many people who used to rely upon their medicines have found it most difficult to demonstrate over their trouble as long as they had at hand the particular material remedy upon which they relied. When they have got rid of their " broken reed " of a support, they have very soon found themselves well. In some cases of which I have known, the healing has been instantaneous. In two cases, directly they threw their drugs out of the window
10 they were well.

Do not Force your Opinion on Others; let Truth Act.

It does not do to force a man out of his belief in material means. As a rule, it is better to let him continue until he sees, himself, that it is a mistake and that he is keeping himself back by taking material steps. The mere fact of ceasing to take material steps, although it is much to be desired, does not change a man's mind. It is the material evidence of the change. The only way in which a man's mind can be changed, so that he leaves his false
20 material basis and works from the spiritual point of view, is either by his praying for himself, or somebody else praying for him. In either case it is equally effective ; but when a man starts to pray for himself his progress is much more rapid, because the amount of time during which God is acting upon him, changing his so-called mind, is much greater than when somebody else is working for him—unless he is not working properly, or is idle. When both are working, naturally the improvement is still quicker.

30 Glorify God.

Prove to a man what you are telling him by the results he sees in you. We must glorify God, not only by being morally and physically better ; but by being mentally more active ; by being more loving, that is to say, considerate and thoughtful for others ; by being wiser, namely, more tactful ; by doing our work and playing our games better ; and by being happier. If we are not happy it means that we do not understand God, who is the Principle of all joy.

40 Experimental Tuition.

In the early days, all my work was more or less

experimental. At first I could not get any of the Christian Scientists to give me any information whatsoever. They thought that, like others, I would make a perfunctory examination into Christian Science, and then bring out a report full of mistakes through not having understood the subject of inquiry. They did not wish me to be able to quote them as having said this, that, or the other, giving a garbled account of what they had said, and they therefore thought it wiser to say nothing. This turned out to be a great advantage to me. Later on it was quite different. I can never be thankful enough for the help received from, and the time ungrudgingly given by, the two Christian Scientists through whose class I went. For some years, nearly every week I used to see them with a list of some thirty or forty questions about things I did not understand. As a rule, after having the first half a dozen questions answered, half the remainder answered themselves.

Be as a Little Child.

As soon as I found what Christian Science was, I chose out the very best Christian Scientist that I could find, and determined to follow her advice implicitly ; and for about three and a half years I did this. " *Whosoever shall not receive the kingdom of God as a little child, he shall not enter therein* " (Mark 10 : 15). Naturally, I do not say she was always right ; in fact, on looking back, I know that mistakes were made ; but, taken on the whole, it was far better for me, and I got on better, and I was much freer from troubles and difficulties than if I had always acted in the way which I myself thought was best. I had all the benefit of her great experience. When I found that she made statements which I knew and had proved were incorrect, and blamed me for trying to get at the higher realization of the truth at which I was aiming, then I knew that the time had come for me to work away by myself. I did not, however, change my previous method of working until I was forced to change. That is to say, I went on attending the Christian Science meetings, and in fact working exactly as previously, until asked not to attend the meetings.

For many years afterwards I was attacked by the Christian Scientists in every shape and way. Lies of

every kind and description were passed on from one to
another. It is only during the last few years that they
have found that the statements made were not true.
Even now in out-of-the-way places, where they have not
learnt the facts, they still make these misstatements.
One of the commonest is that," I obtain my results
by hypnotism." " *Casting out devils by Beelzebub* "
(Luke 11 : 15).

This is the principle upon which to go : Take no steps
until you are forced out of your existing position. If
the new one is better for you, and if you are treating
properly, nothing can keep you in the old position, which
has been outgrown. Whenever you wish to learn anything, it is safer to follow on the lines of the person
teaching until you find that you have lost confidence in
them. Then make a change.

The advice is something like that given by Sir Andrew
Clarke, the famous doctor, in one of his last lectures.
When he was asked his opinion with regard to a new
drug, his reply was : " When a new drug comes out, take
it and run it for all it is worth ; try it for everything.
When you find that it ceases to act in a sufficient number
of cases, then give it up and take the latest new one."
In the words of St. Paul : " *Prove all things ; hold fast
that which is good* " (1 Thess. 5 : 21).

Do what the Other Man wants.

The main principle of life is always to do what the
other man wants. If you find it is something that does
not appeal to you, then treat and rely upon treatment to
make it come out right. If you get your realization
clear enough and have got rid of fear, you will find that
either the man will want you to do something else, or
what he desires you to do will turn out all right. The
reason for this is that whatever you are going to do is
already fixed, and can only be altered with prayer. Fear
shows you that the evil is not sufficiently destroyed with
the treatment. If you press your opinion, you are in-
tensifying the thoughts that are acting. Then they are
more difficult to destroy, should what you want to do not
be the best thing for you to do.

Do Everything by Prayer, not Materially.

You also have to learn to do everything by prayer. Whenever you do a thing materially you are relying upon matter, *alias*, the devil, and not upon God. It is recognized now all over the world that if you think evil you get evil ; when you are thinking of the material world you are thinking evil, as there is nothing really good in the material world ; which latter is heaven hidden by what is called in the Bible "*the veil*" (2 Cor. 3 : 14, 15, 16), *i.e.* the imaginary mist of matter. You cannot do a thing materially without thinking materially ; sometimes it is only a subconscious thought, but as you are thinking of evil, evil follows. If you keep perfectly quiet and pray, you do not intensify the wrong thoughts, and it is easier to get your results, as the wrong thoughts more easily disappear, and you see heaven more as it really is.

The Standard of Good.

At last we have a standard of good. We used to think our only standard of good was our conscience ; we know now that this idea is misleading, as conscience depends almost entirely upon our training. We have now an absolute standard of good, namely, God and heaven.

When there are two things to be done and you are doubtful which is the right one, consider what takes place in heaven, and the thing which is most like what would take place in heaven is the right thing to do. Heaven is an absolute standard of good.

CHAPTER XI

MENTAL SUGGESTION

Proofs that Mental Suggestion is not Used.

WHEN first I started to get results by Right Thinking, the medical men whom I knew said they were obtained merely by mental suggestion, by impressing the patient strongly that he was going to be healed.

The first case which satisfied them that this was not so, was a case of drink. A Christian Scientist came to me to ask for help for her son, a man of over forty years of age, who was drinking himself to death ; he had had nothing but liquor in his room for over a fortnight and was in the last stages of delirium tremens. She told me that she had tried to get help for him from the Christian Scientists, but they had refused on the ground that he had not asked for help. He called himself an Atheist, or an Agnostic, I believe ; at all events, he was very bitter against religion, and especially against Christian Science.

Personal Treatment.

10 The Christian Scientists, in treating, as a rule, realize the spiritual reality of the patient, and in a case of drink, for instance, realize that the patient is not a material man, but is a spiritual being in heaven, who cannot possibly desire drink. As a rule a case is taken personally, that is to say, the practitioner, so to speak, talks silently but mentally to the patient, and says, " You cannot possibly desire drink, for you are a perfect spiritual being in heaven." When treating personally in this way, it is very difficult to prevent thinking a little of the material
20 man. If the patient has asked for help, it is, generally speaking, a sign that his mind is not very bad, and that even if the practitioner does think a little of the material man, it will do no harm. If he has not asked for help, his mind may be very bad, and in some cases, thinking of his so-called material self, even very little, may upset him. Often the practitioner, not understanding what is happening, calls this " chemicalization," which is quite a different thing. The effect of thinking of him is as though a piece of string were tied on to his mind and you
30 were pulling at it. If his mind is very bad and the practitioner thinks a good deal of him, he may be entirely upset.

Impersonal Treatment.

When working in the proper way, whereby one does not think of the person at all, neither of his material self nor of his spiritual reality, no harm of this kind can be done, because the practitioner is treating himself—getting out of his own mind the false idea that man is a material being, sick or sinful as the case may be, and trying to
40 realize the perfection of God and man, the real man.

Instantaneous Healing of Drink Mania.

The Christian Scientist in question told me she had heard that I had taken cases of this sort which had been successful, and asked me to take her son as a patient. I told her I could not do this, as I had too many people waiting at that time, but I would give one treatment; he was at the time in the South of England, and I in my office in the City. He was completely cured at that moment, and about eight years afterwards his mother in passing through London said that she felt she must call and see me to thank me again for what had been done. He had had no difficulties of the kind since, and was a changed man.

When I was attacked by one of the papers advocating spiritualism, they invited any of their readers who had been cured by me to communicate directly with them. I believe they expected to hear of a number of failures. As a matter of fact, the only letter of the kind was from a doctor, who wrote saying a relation of his had not been healed. This was because, after a short time, as the patient would not treat for herself, and would not take any trouble or even try to read, I refused to continue, telling her that as she would not take my medicine, she could not expect it to help her.

Amongst the letters was one from a lady whose husband had suffered from drink for many years, and was getting worse and worse. She wrote to the paper, saying: " I called upon Mr. Rawson and told him, and asked him for help. Mr. Rawson gave an audible treatment, and to my astonishment when I got home I found my husband, who knew nothing of my visit to Mr. Rawson, at dinner, drinking water. Since then he has not touched drink of any kind, and the difference between this and times in the past when by will-power he has forced himself to abstain from drink, is this: he has had no desire of any kind." This was in 1913, and I saw the lady a little time ago and she said that he had had no trouble since. These two instances are enough to prove that the healing is not done by what is now called mental suggestion.

Silent Mental Suggestion.

There is one form of suggestion which is not recognized, except by mental workers, and that is silent mental suggestion. It is almost as effective as when you audibly suggest to a person. This silent mental suggestion was the basis of most of the sorcery and witchcraft of olden times, although it was not known what was being done. Paracelsus, one of the ablest men of olden times, had considerable knowledge of medicine, and was the first to introduce the use of metals as drugs. He took every opportunity he could of learning all about occult matters, 10 and for this purpose used to wander about for months in the company of gipsies and people of the lower grades. For this, amongst other reasons, he fell into disrepute amongst his fellow-workers. In one of his writings he pointed out definitely that the clay figures into which pins were stuck by the witches had nothing to do in any shape or way with the magic and spells and the various incantations they used to chant, but were used so that they could concentrate their mind better upon the part of the victim they wanted to harm. At the same time it 20 must be recognized that the witches were not harming the victims. It was evil thoughts, impersonal evil, attacking both the witches and the victims. Unfortunately in those days people did not know how to pray in the right way so as to protect the victims and change the mind of the witches. Consequently they used to burn anyone whom they thought was practising black art and working in this way. In those days, if you wanted to get rid of an enemy, the simplest way was to hide a brazier, or skull and cross-bones, etc., in their rooms, and then go 30 and lodge a charge against them, saying that they had killed your red-and-white cow, giving it some obviously ridiculous or impossible disease. It helped if you said that you had seen them seated across a broom-stick, flying out of the cowshed at midnight. If you could get someone else to swear it as well, you were certain of a verdict, and the victim was promptly burnt, amongst the howls of those looking on, who went away feeling just as satisfied as many do now when they see a thief caught red-handed and taken off to the police cells.

40   In treatment it is always advisable to work against the effect of mental suggestion, and you can do this by realizing that " there is no mental malpractice, man is surrounded by divine Love ; there is no aggressive mental

suggestion, for there are only God's thoughts; there is
no hypnotism; God is the only power and the only
ruler," etc.

It has often been said that in Christian Science one
does not use mental suggestion. As a matter of fact,
when you are praying personally, that is to say, thinking
of the spiritual reality of the person and talking mentally
to the person, as many do, you are using mental suggestion. When you say, for instance, " You have not got
consumption; your lungs are spiritual and perfect, for 10
you are the son of God, divine, made in God's image and
likeness," you are really using mental suggestion; only
it is not recognized to be this, as a different meaning is
now attached to the words " mental suggestion."

It would be advantageous if a committee were formed
in order to define, as far as possible, the meanings of
the words used by mental workers. It would save a
good deal of the misunderstandings that now necessarily
take place, through the same words being used to
express different ideas.   20

Aggressive Mental Suggestion.

The apparent effect of "aggressive mental suggestion"
has to be recognized and dealt with. Most have heard of
cases where, for a joke, a man's friends have, one after
the other, told him he looked unwell, whereas at first he
was perfectly well, with the result that in a short time he
became ill. Some like myself have heard stories of the
victim dying, as the result of the malpractice. I have
only had one actual case, first hand, of this. A man
came to me in distress. A terrible thing had happened. 30
He did not give me his name or the place where it had
happened, but by the way he spoke it was evidently some
large store or Government department. As a joke, he
said, various members of the staff, one after the other,
had told the head of their department that he looked very
ill, and at ten o'clock the same morning he went home.
To their horror he was dead by one o'clock that day.

Dr. Schofield, the well-known medical authority on
the human mind, told me of a case which he mentions
in one of his books. Two well-known medical men of 40
Edinburgh were arguing as to the effect of mental
suggestion. To prove his case, one of them called to a

man near, and after asking him a question told him that he was looking very ill and ought to go home to bed. He gave him his name and that of his friend, both of them well-known medical men. The man went home to bed, and was dead in a week. The *Daily News*, in reviewing Dr. Schofield's book containing an account of the incident, said that it was a case for the public prosecutor ; that nowadays it was just as much murder to do such a thing as to fire a pistol in a man's face in 10 order to see what effect it would have upon him.*

Foreseeing the Evil and Destroying It.

I remember, after one of the first lectures I ever gave on " how to think rightly," one of the well-known medical specialists came up to me after the meeting and said that for the first time in his life he had had put before him a theory into which all his known facts fitted, and he now saw what a lot of harm he had done in the past. He asked me not to mention his name to anyone, as the medical profession had rather curious views about 20 mental working—and yet he was one of the leaders. He had had a case only that week where a woman had been brought to him for diagnosis. He was the thirteenth medical man she had been to, and none had been able to tell her the cause of her trouble. As the door opened, before even he had seen the woman, he knew, he told me, what the disease was. Within two or three days all the symptoms of the disease came out, caused, he now thought, by his strong thinking that she had this trouble. He thought he had given it to her. As a matter of fact, 30 he had read the thoughts and foreseen the disease. If he had known how to pray rightly he could have stopped it coming, in the same way that a friend of mine destroyed the cinema pictures of the accident in the lane and the bombing of the hospital, as mentioned in the testimony columns of *Active Service* on 4th November 1916, after they had been foreseen by a lady staying in his house. Three members of his household have had this power of seeing the future. I now know about a

* Since this was written, mental suggestion has been recognized by 40 the medical profession, and is largely used. It is always harmful, however, and has been given up on this account by some medical specialists on mental working in London.

hundred who have been able to see the future. Some of them see it constantly, and when evil is foreseen it practically always is destroyed, and the evil does not take place.

Another friend of mine, a well-known medical man, who used to get sometimes as much as £50 for his diagnosis, told me that often he had no apparent reasons for his opinion ; he just knew what the trouble was. He admitted it was thought reading.

On one occasion I went with a leading doctor, who was a specialist on the human mind, to help him to test another doctor, who said he had the power under certain circumstances of reading thought. My friend said he had three things wrong internally, and no one except himself knew what they were. I thereupon treated, knowing that man being spiritual, and God the Principle of all knowledge, man knows instantly everything he needs. At once the other medical man stated accurately what the three troubles were.

Prophesying.

A very noticeable change during the last years has been the great increase in the number of people who can do this. Joel, speaking of the latter days, writes : " And ye shall know that I am in the midst of Israel, and that I am the Lord your God, and none else : and my people shall never be ashamed. And it shall come to pass afterward, that I will pour out my spirit upon all flesh ; and your sons and your daughters shall prophesy, your old men shall dream dreams, your young men shall see visions : And also upon the servants and upon the handmaids in those days will I pour out my spirit. And I will shew wonders in the heavens and in the earth, blood, and fire, and pillars of smoke. The sun shall be turned into darkness, and the moon into blood, before the great and the terrible day of the Lord come. And it shall come to pass, that whosoever shall call on the name of the Lord shall be delivered : for in mount Zion and in Jerusalem shall be deliverance, as the Lord hath said, and in the remnant whom the Lord shall call " (Joel 2 : 27–32).

The first verse is already fulfilled ; we know now that we are the ten tribes of Israel, and that the Lord is our

God and there is nothing but God. The next two verses
are now taking place, as above mentioned. The following two verses show the prophecy of the way in which
the end of the world would come, if it were not for man's
knowledge of how to pray, as not only would the earth
burn up, but "*the heavens*" as well, that is, all the
constellations. As Peter points out when he says, "*The
heavens shall pass away with a great noise*" (this is the
"shout" or "trump" spoken of elsewhere, namely,
the realization that there is nothing but God) "*and the
elements shall melt with fervent heat, the earth also and
the works that are therein shall be burned up.*" Later,
St. Peter says we should be "*looking for and hasting
unto the coming of the day of God, wherein the heavens
being on fire shall be dissolved, and the elements shall melt
with fervent heat.*" "*Dissolve*" is the Biblical name
for "dematerialize," and is used by several of the
prophets in connection with the end of the world. In
the next verse follows the recognition of the prophetic
vision also referred to in Revelation 21 : 1 : "*Nevertheless
we, according to his promise, look for new*" (a doublet of
"now") "*heavens and a new earth, wherein dwelleth
righteousness*" (2 Peter 3 : 10, 12, 13). There are bound to
be preliminary signs of this before what the prophet Joel
speaks of as "*the great and the terrible day of the Lord,*"
which is the final day when the whole universe would
be burned up, which day, or at all events the major
portion of it, will be entirely eliminated by man's prayers.
It is interesting to note that St. Peter, in his account of
the end, does not speak of the "*great and terrible day
of the Lord,*" but of "*that great and notable day of the
Lord*" (Acts 2 : 20). He, like Joel, points out that at
that time "*whosoever shall call on the name of the Lord
shall be saved*" (v. 21).

The final verse in Joel, above quoted, shows the way
in which we are going to be delivered from the troubles
that are now coming upon us. To "*call on the name of
the Lord*" means to realize the nature of God. "*In
mount Zion*" means "in thinking of God," and "*In
Jerusalem*" means "in thinking of heaven." "*The
remnant whom the Lord shall call*" are those of the
children of Israel, or English-speaking races, whose minds
are sufficiently spiritual to recognize the second coming

of Christ, now coming " *like lightning* " all over the world, and to hear the voice of God calling, " *Come out from among them, and be ye separate* " (2 Cor. 6 : 17).

CHAPTER XII

PERSONAL AND IMPERSONAL TREATMENT

I AM continually being asked whether it is right to treat for a person without their consent. The reason for this is that the Christian Science practitioners refuse to treat a person without their consent ; in fact, they think it absolutely wrong to do such a thing. There is a very 10 sound reason for this. Some years ago the regular method at Christian Science classes was to teach the student to think of the spiritual reality of the patient ; that is to say, to think of the patient as an absolutely perfect being in heaven. This I call personal treatment to distinguish it from the method, which I have always adopted, of not thinking of the person at all, but trying to realize as clearly as I can the facts in connection with God and man, man specifically, namely, God's infinite consciousness.   20

When working in this way one is not treating the patient, but treating oneself, that is, treating *for* the patient.

The Evolution of Divine Healing.

It has to be recognized that divine healing has been a matter of steady growth. At one time I was told it was the practice to sit back to back, imagining that in some way there was an electric current passing from one spine to the other. This probably came from the old idea which Mesmer enunciated, namely, that electricity flowed to the 30 patients from the tips of his fingers and healed them. Later on, people used the human mind, and thought of a perfect human being whom they located in heaven. They thought, for instance, of a perfect heart, or a perfect leg, as the case might be, not recognizing that the mere fact of thinking of outline, shape, and form—as material beings know them—as existing in heaven, did not get away from the material limited concept of man. Whenever you are thinking of the material world you are thinking of evil, and evil invariably follows.

I remember once being asked to treat for one of the well-known lecturers and practitioners, not a Christian Scientist, who could not get away from her own troubles. After a short talk I told her that her difficulty was that she was still on a material basis. This she indignantly denied. I then asked her how she would treat for a person who had a weak heart. She answered : " I would
10 turn in thought to heaven, and I would realize a perfect man with an absolutely perfect heart, having all power and strength and beating rhythmically." Any result gained in this way is purely hypnotic, and the result of the action of the human mind. It is not true healing at all, as some trouble must come back later on.

As I have pointed out in *Life Understood*, the heart is the reflection of God as Love, and Love is omnipotent, for God is Love. The sufficiently clear realization of this would instantly cure any weak heart in the world,
20 not because you have done anything, but because you have got right away from matter and material things, allowing—from a theological point of view—the action of God to take place and destroy the evil that was the cause of the trouble.

In the case mentioned, the result of working the wrong way was that, knowing the effect of thought, directly the symptoms of any trouble arose, the patient could not get away from worrying over the trouble, neither could she think in the way she did, as above mentioned, of a
30 perfect organ in heaven.

Fear kept on Intruding.

Instead of getting away altogether from the material world and thinking only of God, of absolute good, she had an intense fear of what was going to happen. She knew all the symptoms of the various diseases, and, directly she had a twinge in any particular part, she was sure that some particular disease was starting to attack her. Not being able to think of the perfection of that particular organ or limb, she was certain that the
40 trouble was coming. It was a pitiable sight. She was a clever, loving woman, and yet wrong mental working had brought her to this state. Fortunately she soon got

over her troubles. This is the nature of evil, to bring about its own destruction.

Personal Treatment.

Later on, when the Christian Scientists began to understand Mrs. Eddy's writings, there was a considerable advance made, and people did their best to think of the spiritual reality of the patient, free from any limited material ideas. In the year 1901, when I was investigating Christian Science for the *Daily Express*, as far as I know, practically everyone was working in the old way, and I certainly discussed the question with the principal workers. Some of them were even on a much more material basis than this. I remember asking one of the practitioners, who was librarian at the time, for a book, when she replied that she could not attend to me, as she was afraid that she would miss her train. I then replied that I hoped that she had reversed this. She said, " Of course I did ; if it is right I shall catch my train." I could not make her see that this latter thought was not true prayer, and had solely an hypnotic effect. The only result was that she told others that I did not understand Christian Science. The true method of working is to realize that man never misses any train ; he is always in the right place and goes instantly from idea to idea. It is always wrong to think in any way of the material world except to deny its existence.

Impersonal Treatment.

Lately, since it has been made so very clear that one should not think of the person at all, but should think solely of God and heaven, or of the ideal man, many of the Christian Scientists have fortunately changed their method of working, and are treating in what I call an impersonal way. I hope that soon they will begin to realize in their treatments the spiritual realities of the different parts of the body. An article has appeared in one of their papers, saying that all treatment is impersonal, and that there is no such thing as personal treatment. I have found on cross-examination of their practitioners that even the leaders have not really got clearly in their minds the difference between what I call personal and impersonal treatment. In any case, the expressions are useful, so as to discriminate between what I call the highest, and the inferior method of divine healing. The objection to personal treatment, as it has been defined above, is that when you are treating, you have a sort of sense of the mentality of the patient, and this sense may develop into an actual mechanical action upon the human consciousness of the individual thought of. This happens when a person thinks of the human patient instead of the ideal spiritual man, and thinks so vividly that he actually sees the material face, or even the material body. This may be called picturing, and corresponds to the black magic mentioned by Ezekiel in chapter 8 : 12, where he says, " *Hast thou seen what the ancients of the house of Israel do in the dark, every man in the chambers of his imagery ?* " The punishment of these men is shown in verses 2 and 8 of the succeeding chapter.

CHAPTER XIII

THE MOVEMENT OF MATTER

Permanency the Test of Reality.

IN *Healing by the Realization of God, or True Prayer for Doctors,** a pamphlet written at the request of various medical readers of *Active Service*, I give seven different ways of looking at the material world, with the advantages arising from understanding these different points of view.

The first is the religious view as set out in the Bible ; the second, the metaphysical view, adopted by those who look upon everything material as something subjective, or a concept in one's own mind. The material world is, so viewed, simply our false concept of heaven ; if, therefore, we change our concept, the thing changes more or less in accordance with our concept ; the third is the view that Buddha put forward, that the material world is a dream, but we find that it is a dream without a dreamer ; the fourth, that we are hypnotized into our troubles ; the

* *Healing by the Realization of God, or True Prayer for Doctors* (Second Edition), 2s. net, postage 2d. Published by The S.S.K.T.P.

The Society for Spreading the Knowledge of True Prayer

14a, Eccleston Street, London, S.W.I, England.

fifth, the natural science point of view, that thought is a high-tension current right above the Marconi wave, and that every sin and disease has a different rate of vibration ; thus if the respective sin or disease cell in the subconscious mind is not sufficiently purified, it vibrates when the thoughts attack, and one has the sin or disease, as the case may be. The sixth point of view is that heaven is a world of four dimensions, of which we see only three, and therefore see it all wrongly. The seventh is that all the good we see around us is part of heaven, made by God, and is permanent and eternal, and that all the evil is best described as a series of pictures seeming to flash by at the rate of about twenty miles an hour, about ten or twelve pictures per second, hiding heaven from us.

Whilst these methods of looking at the material world are of use in understanding better how to overcome the evil around us, none of them are absolutely true, as there is only one true thing which can be said about the material world and evil—namely, that they do not exist. This means that they have no permanency, no reality. Nothing can be real unless it is permanent. As Herbert Spencer has said, " What is real is permanent ; what is not real is not permanent." This is the only true test of reality. It is an axiom that nothing which ever did not exist can exist now, to exist being the same as to be real and permanent. Zeno, who has been called by Aristotle, the Father of Logic, and who obtained his knowledge from that marvellous man Pythagoras, said, *Ex nihilo nihil fit*. In other words, nothing can be made out of nothing. Many of Zeno's marvellously logical statements used to amaze me. One of these statements is that if time and space are infinitely divisible, then motion is an illusion of the senses. He also said that a flying arrow is at every moment of its flight stationary in one particular spot. Before I started my investigation into mental working, I never could understand how matter could move at all, and could never get anyone to explain it. If you move any particular object, say an arrow, at one moment it is there, in its place, and when you have moved it away it is not there. These are the only two known conditions. Either it is there or it is not there. I never could understand how a thing could move from being " there " to being " not there."

Why Matter appears to Move.

Later I found that the movement of matter is due to a succession of dematerializations and materializations. The arrow, for instance, dematerializes in one position and is materialized closer at hand ; it is dematerialized again and materialized a little farther on, so that the succession of dematerializations and materializations looks like an arrow moving. It will be seen, therefore, that Zeno's logical deduction about the flying arrow was
10 perfectly correct. These successive appearances are best described as a number of cinematographic pictures that appear successively to pass. As far as anything in the material world can be said to exist, they existed thousands of years ago. That is, there being no such thing as time, they were all there and all disappear at the same moment.

Eight years after I had found that this was the best way of looking at the material world, giving least power to matter or evil, I found that Emanuel Kant, whom nine out of ten thinkers look upon as the greatest
20 philosopher of modern times, who revolutionized modern philosophy, said in his *Inaugural Dissertation :* " This world's life is only an appearance, a sensuous image of the pure spiritual life, and the whole world of sense only a picture swimming before our present knowing faculty, like a dream, and having no reality itself. For if we should see things and ourselves as they are, we should see ourselves in a world of spiritual natures with which our entire real relation neither began at birth nor ended with the body's death." *

30 So material has the world in general become that people have quite lost sight of the fact that in the past the non-reality of matter and of the material world was taught by many great thinkers. Not only is it frequently referred to in the Old Testament (*e.g.* Isa. 41 : 24 ; 34 : 12 ; 40 : 17 ; Dan. 4 : 35 ; 1 Esdras 6 : 56 ; Amos 6 : 13), but St. Paul in Gal. 6 : 3 writes : " *If a man think himself to be something, when he is nothing,* he *deceiveth himself.*" He also says : " *The things which are*

* " The Quantum Theory " recently put forward, in the words of
40 one of the most eminent English scientific men, " proves that we have a cinematographic existence, consisting of a series of discontinuous jumps. We shall have," he says, " to revise all our existing conceptions of time and space."

*seen are temporal ; but the things which are not seen are
eternal* " (2 Cor. 4 : 18). This means that the material
world is not real, for it is axiomatic in natural science
that anything which ever did not exist or which ceases
to exist is not real, whatever it may appear to be.

St. Augustine, in his soliloquies, writes : " Without
Him was nothing made ; for without the sovereign Good
there is no good. But that is evil, in which there is no
good, and consequently it is nothing, because evil is
nothing but the absence of good." This is not an isolated [10]
instance ; several times he refers to it. For instance, he
says : " Evil is therefore nothing ; because it was made
without the Word, without whom nothing was made."

Origen also wrote : " Seeing evil nowhere exists, for
God is all things, and to Him no evil is near."

Luther also taught the non-reality of evil, and re-
garded " the visible world as an illusion, essentially evil
and misleading."

Natural science has found out that matter can be
caused to cease its apparent existence, and soon it will [20]
be found that it can be caused to appear by thought ; in
fact, that, as Huxley pointed out, it is merely mental
phenomena, and is, as Professor Ostwald says : " Only a
thing imagined, which we have constructed for ourselves
very imperfectly to represent the constant element in
the changing series of phenomena."

The great thinkers of the past also taught the non-
reality of matter. For instance, Euclid said that evil is
only an illusion of our sensuous natures, and has no real
existence. [30]

Matter Proved Mathematically to be Unreal.

When I had almost finished my examination for the
Daily Express, I saw that the only thing that remained
was to prove mathematically the non-reality of matter.
Previously, during my examination, when I had wanted
anything of the kind, I treated, realizing, for instance,
that " God is the Principle of all knowledge, and therefore that man (*i.e.* spiritual man) knows instantly everything he needs," and so obtained the required knowledge.
In this case I was afraid, because I knew that I had not [40]
sufficient mathematical knowledge myself to work it out.
I was afraid because up to that time I was able to say

that I had not had a failure in anything of the kind of any importance, and I feared failing in this respect at the end. At last the thought came to me, " Now, here you are, breaking one of your first principles by allowing yourself to be afraid." So I made up my mind to treat for the knowledge. I expected, as a matter of fact, that either my head chemist or my head engineer, both first-class mathematicians, would work it out for me. I treated five times during two days, realizing that God is the Principle of all knowledge, and that, therefore, man knows instantly anything he needs. The following morning I received from Mr. Wake-Cook a copy of the Rede Lecture, given by Professor Osborne Reynolds, showing that he had proved mathematically the non-reality of matter. I was much interested to find that he had proved mathematically what I had already found to be the case, namely, that the movement of matter is a constant succession of materializations and dematerializa-tions. This also fits in with the cinematograph-picture view of matter, because the apparent movement is simply the flashing by of separate cinema pictures, each a little separate from the previous one. Although the pictures do not move, and we merely run along them, so to speak, it is easier to follow what takes place if the pictures are spoken of as moving.

Millions of years ago, at the so-called start of the material world, all these cinema pictures were in their place just as the photographic pictures are on the film that passes through the lantern. Equally they are bound to be made manifest at their appointed time. Fatalism would be true were it not that these pictures are always slowly automatically improving ; rapidly when we are thinking of God and of heaven. It has always been difficult for those who are naturally able to read the future, to foretell the time when these cinema pictures of the future will appear. It can, however, be accurately done by true prayer.

CHAPTER XIV

PREDESTINATION AND FATALISM

I DEAL fully with the question of the non-reality of matter, and the evolution of my knowledge of the various proofs thereof, in a pamphlet called *The Non-Reality of Matter*, which is an account of a lecture I delivered on this subject at a meeting of the International New Thought Alliance in London.*

Predestination is True.

I think that I might deal here with the question of predestination and fatalism. Predestination, as St. Paul pointed out, is true; fatalism is untrue.

Sir William Smith, in his well-known *Dictionary of the Bible*, in dealing with the question of prayer, refers to the problem as follows : " Scripture does not give any theoretical explanation of the mystery which attaches to prayer. The difficulty of understanding its real efficacy arises chiefly from two sources : from the belief that man lives under general laws, which in all cases must be fulfilled unalterably ; and the opposing belief that he is master of his own destiny, and need pray for no external blessing. The first difficulty is even increased when we substitute the belief in a Personal God for the sense of an Impersonal Deity ; since not only does the predestination of God seem to render prayer useless, but His wisdom and love, giving freely to man all that is good for him, appear to make it needless."

Fatalism is not True.

I believe the reason why the fact of predestination has not been generally admitted is that people have failed to make any distinction between predestination and fatalism. Predestination means that everything that takes place was there at the so-called start of the material world, but has steadily been improved since the beginning, and is being steadily improved still—slowly when we do

* *The Non-Reality of Matter*. Price 4d., postage 1d. Published by The S.K.T.P. Book & Publishing Dept., 12 Buckingham Palace Gardens.

The Society for Spreading the Knowledge of True Prayer

14a, Eccleston Street, London, S.W.1, England.

not pray, rapidly when we pray, prayer being the sign that this improvement is taking place. Fatalism is the belief that everything that happens is bound to happen, and cannot be changed. It is quite true that whatever happens cannot be changed by the human mind, or by what is called will-power. If you speak to a confirmed drunkard he will tell you he has done everything to stop himself from drinking and has failed. Even Paul wrote :
" *For what I would, that do I not : but what I hate, that do I* '" (Rom. 7 : 15). The only way in which you can alter the future is by true prayer, by turning in thought to God and His manifestation, heaven. Then an improvement not only takes place, but *must* take place. The only question is only one of degree. We cannot tell, however, what will happen. In about seventy-five cases out of a hundred your demonstration will be what you expect. In about twenty per cent. something different will occur. With a good worker, about five per cent. are failures, the difficulty being more than the person praying can overcome in the time.

We all know, or ought to know, that what a man does at any moment is governed by what he thinks, as even when there is unpremeditated action, there are subconscious thoughts, the apparent cause of it. These thoughts are similar to those that make you move your feet one after the other when you walk, that keep your heart beating, etc. It has also been recognized that we do not make these thoughts, but that they come to us, or strike us, as it is called. Mr. Arthur Balfour, once Prime Minister, and a deep thinker (now Earl Balfour), in *Mind* of October 1893, wrote as follows : " Whether it be proper to call him free or not, he at least lacks freedom in the sense in which freedom is necessary in order to establish responsibility. It is impossible for him to say that he ' ought ' and therefore he ' can,' for at any given moment of his life his next action is, by hypothesis, strictly determined." This hypothesis is now very generally accepted, and is put in this way : What a man does is dependent upon his environment. It now turns out that everything is hypothetical except the will of God.

It is not long ago that the Church taught that a few beings were destined to be saved and the remainder were destined to be damned, and no man could in any way change from one group to the other.

St. Paul pointed out the difference between pre-destination and fatalism. He said : *" For whom he did foreknow, he also did predestinate to be conformed to the image of his Son, that he might be the firstborn among many brethren. Moreover whom he did predestinate, them he also called ; and whom he called, them he also justi-fied ; and whom he justified, them he also glorified "* (Rom. 8 : 29, 30). *"In whom also we have obtained an inheritance, being predestinated according to the purpose of him who worketh all things after the counsel of his own will : that we should be to the praise of his glory "* (Eph. 1 : 11, 12). *" For by grace are ye saved through faith ; and that not of yourselves : it is the gift of God "* (Eph. 2 : 8).

Our Lord made it perfectly clear that a man could not even pray unless the action of God takes place on him. He said : *" No man can come to me, except the Father which hath sent me draw him "* (John 6 : 44). Dean Inge, the Dean of St. Paul's, has written : " The motive power is not in ourselves. We cannot even will to please God without the help of His will. The experiences of the saints, as recorded by themselves, offer no support to a voluntaristic psychology of religion" (*Personal Idealism and Mysticism*, p. 145). Other confirmations of this view in the Bible are as follows : *" Blessed is the man whom thou choosest, and causest to approach unto thee, that he may dwell in thy courts "* (Ps. 65 : 4) ; *" God ; Who hath saved us, and called us with an holy calling, not according to our works, but according to his own purpose and grace, which was given us in Christ Jesus before the world began "* (2 Tim. 1 : 8, 9) ; *" for by grace are ye saved . . . it is the gift of God "* (Eph. 2 : 8). There are some half a dozen other passages to the same effect ; and this is why our Lord, in his supreme moment on the cross, said : *" My God, my God, why hast thou forsaken me ? "* (Matt. 27 : 46).

CHAPTER XV

GRACE AND THE SECOND COMING OF THE CHRIST

Grace.

MANY do not know what grace is. It is the action of God on you that makes you treat. This action of God is the same as the action of the Holy Ghost or the Holy Spirit. Many people laugh at the idea of the Trinity, God the Father, God the Son, and God the Holy Ghost, or Holy Spirit. When you come to under-
10 stand the meaning of the words, you will find that they are perfectly scientific. God the Father we all recognize; that is to say, God is incorporeal, everlasting Life; ever-present omnipotent Truth, unfolding its own immortal ideas; inexhaustible, perfect Love; self-existent, unfathomable Mind; divine and sinless Soul; supreme, infinite Spirit; the unerring and only intelligence; divine substance, which gives all permanence; and last, but not least, Principle—the Principle of all law and order, the Principle of all good.
20 The total manifestation of God is God the Son, the only begotten of the Father. God, the Holy Spirit, has been much more difficult to understand, and many ideas have been put forward, most of them based upon the facts of the material world instead of the facts of the spiritual world, the world of reality.

God the Holy Spirit.

God the Holy Spirit is the action of God on man—the real man—that makes man what he is, namely, the knowledge or consciousness or thinking of God. God thinks,
30 and the ideas move. This movement is man, or God's thinking; in other words, man is the movement of God's ideas in Mind. The Holy Spirit, therefore, is the action of God that makes the spiritual man think of God.

The Holy Ghost.

We see this action through the mist of matter, and see it in a limited way. This limited action is called the Holy Ghost; in other words, the Holy Ghost is the action of God that makes the material man think of God, or pray in the right way, namely, by the realization of God.

True or scientific prayer is the incoming of the Holy Ghost, which reveals and explains God's universe. It is the kingdom of God, which, whilst continually resulting in a man who has accepted the second coming of the Christ, praying, I believe comes only once in its seeming fullness to a man, until he can heal practically everything instantaneously, but which, when it comes in its fullness, leaves him with the knowledge of what John meant 10 when he wrote : " *I was in the Spirit on the Lord's day* " (Rev. 1 : 10), " *And I saw a new heaven and a new earth : that great city, the holy Jerusalem, descending out of heaven from God, having the glory of God* " (Rev. 21 : 1, 10, 11). Dr. Inge writes : " This idea, that the Holy Ghost is the copula, who ' in perfect love dost join the Father and the Son,' is not, as is usually supposed, an original speculation of Augustine's, but is found in Victorinus, to whom he owes so much " (*The Paddock Lectures for* 1906). " Our Lord imposed no rigorous ceremonies on 20 his disciples. He taught them to enter into the closet, to retire within the heart, to speak but few words ; to open their hearts to receive the descent of the Holy Spirit " (Madame de Guyon). It is the action of the Holy Ghost or Holy Comforter, the Spirit of Truth, of which John speaks as follows : " *If ye love me, keep my commandments. And I will pray the Father, and he shall give you another Comforter, that he may abide with you for ever ; Even the Spirit of truth ; whom the world cannot receive, because it seeth him not, neither knoweth him : but ye* 30 *know him ; for he dwelleth with you and shall be in you. At that day ye shall know that I am in my Father, and ye in me, and I in you* " (John 14 : 15, 16, 20).

My readers will by this time have got clearly into their minds the difference between true prayer, which is conscious communion with God—the realization of the highest good of which man is capable of thinking—and supplicatory prayer, which is choosing what one thinks is good for one's self or for one's fellow-man, and having absolute faith that it is going to happen. This, as will 40 have been seen, is hypnotic, and is harmful in many cases, although it is true that when one is asking God to do anything, as one thinks of God, the action of God takes place and helps the supplicant. The length of time during which one is thinking of God is so short, as a rule, that there is but little result therefrom. Sometimes, however, wonderful results have been obtained in this way, so clear has been the realization.

The Second Coming of Christ.

In John 14 : 20 we find that Jesus, after saying that the Holy Ghost or Comforter was coming, followed on by saying : " *At that day ye shall know that I am in my Father, and ye in me, and I in you.*"

The recognition of this fact, that there is nothing but God and His manifestation, is due to the second coming of Christ. In verse 26 we read as follows : " *But the Comforter, which is the Holy Ghost, whom the Father will send in my name, he shall teach you all things, and bring all things to your remembrance, whatsoever I have said unto you.*" It is the mental realization of the truth that comes with the healing, and the Holy Ghost is the spirit or holiness of this truth, that abides " *with you for ever,*" and heals and " *shall teach you all things.*" What is necessary, to see conscious healing, is to learn how to pray scientifically and how to demonstrate the Christ-life, and so by increasing holiness to become a consecrated channel for spiritual good.

Dr. R. F. Horton, the well-known Congregational minister, has stated that " the whole trend of the advanced scholarship of our time is to declare that the main teaching of Christ is the Apocalyptic Return " ; in other words, the second coming of Christ. This is correct, and I believe that the main point in his teachings was to show us how to destroy the evils which were coming at what is called the end of the world, namely, as all matter disappears. He must have known that the world would be too material to understand his teachings.

The Sermon on the Mount, Liveable.

Until quite recently the Sermon on the Mount, as given in the 5th chapter of St. Matthew's Gospel, could not be lived, and yet it is probably his most important message. Now that we know how to pray we can live it. We have to do what the other man wants, and if one prays properly until fear is gone, it will be found that this is the best thing for him and for you. If there is fear it means that there is evil ahead, and one has to treat until the fear has gone.

Our Lord, in answer to the request of the disciples, pointed out when the end of the world should come, and gave the signs of the end. These are being steadily fulfilled. The end of the world is dealt with by nearly all the prophets, and they are unanimous in pointing out that those who know how to pray rightly are not to have any troubles of any kind, not even fear. On the contrary, they will be absolutely joyous ; not only from the knowledge of the fact that all troubles are shortly disappearing, and that everyone is about to wake up and find themselves perfect beings in a perfect world ; but because they are continually helping their fellow-men out of suffering, and freeing them from their troubles. These become worse and worse as we approach the end of matter.

CHAPTER XVI

JESUS THE CHRIST

" But Whom say Ye that I am ? "

WE know now that the word "Christ" has many different interpretations. Many think that the Christ was the material or human being Jesus—" *the man Christ Jesus* " (1 Tim. 2 : 5), as Paul says, and many think that Jesus was called the Christ to show that he was part of God. Some people actually believe that God left His world that He had created, and came down to earth and was seen as a material man. This is simply a remnant of the old pagan teaching that the gods could, at times, leave the heavens and come down and consort with mankind. Jesus pointed out that the Christ is no localized individual, but is as infinite as God. He said, speaking of the present days : " *Then if any man shall say unto you, Lo, here is Christ, or there ; believe it not* " (Matt. 24 : 23).

We now know that God is " *all in all,*" and there is nothing but God and His manifestation, which we see all falsely.

When we study the Bible to find out the meaning of the Christ, we find there are two distinct uses of the word. The first is the title given to our Lord : Jesus the Christ. He was the only man entitled to this honour.

The Final End of the Material Man.

Many men, I believe, ultimately so purified themselves that, like the Master, they dematerialized their human minds and bodies and disappeared for ever from the sight of the material beings amongst whom they had dwelt.

10 Not only have we the actual records of Elijah and our Lord, but we have the inferential statements with regard to Enoch and Melchizedek. The body of John, the beloved disciple, was never found, and there is no record of his death. The same remark applies to Moses, who—notwithstanding the terrible mistake he made when he used his human mind and struck the rock the second time, when water rushed forth through his resorting to the old black magic methods of the Egyptians—was a marvellous man. I believe that Gautama Buddha also 20 dematerialized. There are two accounts of his end. The usual one is impossible. A man with even the knowledge that many have to-day could not possibly have spoken and acted in the way stated. The other account is, I believe, correct. According to this, he left his followers and went up into a mountain and made a cave his resting-place. For about ten days they brought him rice and water, and put it outside. One day they found the food still in its place ; entering the cave there was no sign of their beloved teacher to be found, nor was any 30 trace of him ever discovered.

The same is said to have been the end of Lao-Tse, also a wonderful teacher who lived about the same time as Buddha. Telling his disciples not to follow him, he went outside the city and up into a mountain. As he had not returned the next day they followed him, but like Elijah, Buddha, and Moses, they were never able to find any trace of him.

Scientifically, this would be the only end of men with such a knowledge of the truth. Once a man has recog-40 nized the second coming of the Christ, it is only a question of time before he gets rid, first, of all worries and troubles, then of all disease, next of sin, then of limitations.

Later his material body is dematerialized, and finally his material or carnal mind disappears. Then the man ascending into heaven, as it is called, appears.

Jesus the Christ.

The real man, the Son of God, always was and always will be a perfect being, in a perfect world, governed by a perfect God, " *in Christ*." Apart from his virgin birth, the difference between Jesus and these other men, and one reason why he was the only one entitled to be called the Christ, is that he, instead of going away quietly and dematerializing as the others did, took his place right in the forefront of the battle and fought evil to the very last.

He could have gone away quietly some years before he actually dematerialized, and could have steadily worked away, recognizing his unity with the Father, until at last even his human mind disappeared, as it did at the ascension. He would not then have run the terrible risk that he did of perhaps not being able to protect himself against the death thought, so that it would cause him to pass on, to work out the problem in the next state of consciousness.

The Object of our Lord's Ministry.

Our Lord had a difficult problem to solve. How was he to speak and live so that when the time came and the world was good enough—that is, unselfish enough—to be enabled to understand what he taught, it would recognize his position, understand his message, and start to follow in his footsteps ?

He knew well enough, none knew better, the date on which this material world, this throbbing hell, was coming to its predestined end.

When " *the disciples came unto him privately, saying, Tell us, when shall these things be ?* " (Matt. 24 : 3), our Lord replied as follows : " *When ye therefore shall see the abomination of desolation, spoken of by Daniel the prophet, stand in the holy place*," and added (" *whoso readeth let him understand :* ") (ver. 15). He replied thus, for, as I have shown in *Active Service* of 26th August and 22nd September 1920, the prophecies of Daniel show that he knew very closely the date of the so-called end of the world, the end of matter, which is the end of all sin, disease, and limitation. He did not know the actual day or the hour, as is mentioned in Mark 13 : 32, which reads as follows : " *But of that day and that hour knoweth no man, no, not the angels which are in heaven, neither the Son, but the Father.*" He did not say we should not know the week or the year. I am sure that he knew both of these, but not the day and hour. The words " *knoweth no man* " means that you cannot calculate the time mathematically or astrologically. " *Not the angels* " means that you cannot get it by treatment, namely, by the angels Michael and Gabriel—the denial and the affirmation. " *Neither the Son* " means that he did not know himself, and " *but the Father* " means that the actual day and hour depend entirely upon the action of God, and is shown by the way in which we pray. If we do our work well and accurately now, it ought not to last twenty-four hours, but if we do our work badly or carelessly it might last for several days. Our Lord said in the 20th verse of the same chapter : " *And except that the Lord had shortened those days, no flesh should be saved : but for the elect's sake, whom he hath chosen, he hath shortened the days.*" " *The elect* " is the Bible name given to those who know how to pray rightly—namely, by the realization of God.

Jesus knew well enough the terrible scenes through which the world is about to pass in its death throes, and described them in these telling words : " *For then shall be great tribulations, such as was not since the beginning of the world to this time, no nor ever shall be* " (Matt. 24 : 21). Daniel used almost the same words when he said : " *There shall be a time of trouble, such as never was since there was a nation even to that same time* " (Dan. 12 : 1).

One of His Objects was to Reduce this Terrible Suffering.

Our Lord knew and, with his marvellous love, allowed for the materiality that was going to bind humanity down to its rock of Prometheus. He saw the punishment his disciples were about to receive on account of their materiality, which had caused them to flee when they thought their beloved Master had failed in his mission. The latter, they thought, was to establish a material world-wide kingdom of the Jews. Even the beloved John, just before our Lord went for the last time up to Jerusalem, asked whether fire should be called down from heaven on those who differed from their views. "*The Samaritans . . . did not receive him, because his face was as though he would go to Jerusalem. And when his disciples James and John saw this, they said, Lord, wilt thou that we command fire to come down from heaven, and consume them, even as Elias did ? But he turned, and rebuked them, and said, Ye know not what manner of spirit ye are of. For the Son of man is not come to destroy men's lives, but to save them*" (Luke 9 : 52, 54–56).

As I have pointed out, in several places in the Bible it is shown that the disciples used the human mind in their healing. This was the case even right at the end, and several times Jesus reproved them for praying in this way. They did not get to a spiritual basis until after he had made his unparalleled demonstration and come out of the tomb. The above is another of the places where it is shown that the action of God, through true prayer, could not possibly have resulted in the burning of the Samaritans. Further, they must have been used to doing things of this nature, or otherwise they would not have asked Jesus whether he *desired* them to do such a dreadful thing.

The same evil stalks rampant amongst the religions of to-day. It has covered itself with a cloak of respectability, but is just as cruel as when it tortured its victims on the rack and burnt those who were striving to escape from its toils. Even the once persecuted, although not entirely free from persecution, is driven by this evil to prevent those whom it thinks are wrong, from helping their fellow-men to a new and better view of Truth. To-day it tries to instil poisoned words into the minds of its victims and lifts its garish robe lest it might touch the mental field of the lowly disciple. With the cry : "*Art thou come hither to torment us before the time ?*" (Matt. 8 : 29), it would equally desire fire to remove those with whom it differed could they not otherwise be quieted.

CHAPTER XVII

THE MYSTIC CHRIST

The Mystic Christ.

THE other meaning usually attached to the word
" *Christ* " is what people speak of as " the mystic
Christ." Some by this mean that it is not exactly known
what this " *Christ* " is, but others speak of it in this way,
having a definite understanding of what they consider
the word means, although not being able to explain what
10 their idea of Christ is, or to realize it clearly.

Taken generally, this second meaning is variously
classified—*e.g.* the meaning attached to it by St. Paul ;
the meaning attached to it in the Church by the more
spiritual theologians ; the meaning given by Mrs. Eddy ;
and a fifth meaning, which is one that I often give to
it myself in treatment.

Both St. John and St. Paul have pointed out that
we are " *in Christ.*" They looked upon the Christ as all
the spiritual beings in heaven together. " *Blessed . . .*
20 *with all spiritual blessings in the heavenly places in
Christ* " (Eph. 1 : 3).

" *We, being many, are one body in Christ* " (Rom.
12 : 5) ; " *we are in . . . Jesus Christ* " (1 John 5 : 20).
" *Your bodies are the members of Christ* " (1 Cor. 6 : 15).
" *In Christ shall all be made alive* " (1 Cor. 15 : 22).
" *Your life is hid with Christ in God* " (Col. 3 : 3).
" *The church, which is his body, the fulness of him that
filleth all in all* " (Eph. 1 : 22, 23). Remember that
" church " means originally, " an assembly " (Smith's
30 *Dictionary of the Bible*, vol. i. page 594).

As the Rev. Charles Kingsley said : " Union with
Christ must be something real and substantial, and
not merely a metaphor and a flower of rhetoric." St.
Augustine said : " Let us rejoice and return thanks that
we have been made, not only Christians, but Christ."

Views of the Church of England.

Dean Inge, Dean of St. Paul's, and late Professor of
Divinity at Cambridge, in *The Paddock Lectures for*
1906, writes : " Union with the glorified Christ is the

essence of Christianity." Professor Wallace, of Oxford, says : " The great deed that seems to emerge as the life of Christ is the bringing into one of God and man." This is also the main point in the teachings of Mrs. Eddy.

One of Mrs. Eddy's teachings is that it is the realization of the Christ that heals, and she speaks of the Christ as " the divine manifestation of God which comes to the flesh to destroy incarnate error " (*S. & H.*, p. 583, l. 10). Dean Inge confirms this, and says : " The realization of this conception heals sin and sickness." Later, he says : [10] " I will collect the chief passages which, taken together, comprise St. Paul's teaching on this subject. In relation to God the Father, Christ is the Image (eikon) of God (2 Cor., Col.) . . . An eikon . . . represents its prototype, and is a visible manifestation of it. Christ is the ' eikon of the Invisible God ' (Col.). In him dwells bodily the Pleroma, the totality of the Divine attributes (Col., Eph.). He is ' Lord of all ' and ' Lord of Glory ' (Rom., 1 Cor.). ' In reference to the world, Christ is the Agent in creation, through Him are all things, and [20] we through Him ' (1 Cor. 8 : 6). . . . He is ' the first-born of all creation ; in Him and through Him and unto Him are all things. He is before all things, and in Him all things hold together ' (Col. 1 : 15, 16). ' All things are to be summed up in Him ' (Eph. 1 : 10). ' Christ is all, and in all ' (Col. 3 : 11). His reign is co-extensive with the world's history. ' He must reign till He hath put all His enemies under His feet. The last enemy that shall be abolished is death.' "

Archdeacon Wilberforce writes : " When we recognize [30] . . . that the mystic Christ is in all, and that every human being is a potential Jesus, we have realized what it is to be ' *in the Lord.*' If only we could stand fast in the truth ! "

The Christ is as infinite as God, the expression of God, " *of whom are all things, and we in him* " (1 Cor. 8 : 6). We, therefore, individualize the power or activity of God, for God is seen to work by means of specific man, *the Christ.* " *Christ the power of God, and the wisdom of God* " (1 Cor. 1 : 24). " *His eternal power and God-* [40] *head* " (Rom. 1 : 20). This is " the mystic Christ " of the early Fathers (see Eph. 3 : 3, 5, 9).

It is this mystery that Paul speaks of as follows :

" *Continue in prayer . . . withal praying also for us, that God would open unto us a door of utterance, to speak the mystery of Christ* " (Col. 4 : 2, 3).

The Christ being the true idea of God, this " *mystery of Christ* " is now solved, as, not only do we know what God is, but we can prove what God is.

That this would be so was prophesied in Revelation 10 : 7, as follows : " *But in the days of the voice of the seventh angel, when he shall begin to sound, the mystery of God should be finished, as he hath declared to his servants the prophets.*" There is no longer any mystery as to what God, the Christ, the Holy Spirit, the Holy Ghost, or the Logos are, and a man can prove the truth of his knowledge by the results that follow his realizations.

A Roman Catholic View.

Father Tyrrell, in *The Way of Truth*. writes : " The oneness of all men with one another in Christ, and their oneness with God through Christ, is the foundation of all practical and effective religion."

Christian Science Views.

Christian Science teaches that Christ expresses God's spiritual eternal nature and is the divinity or spiritual selfhood of Jesus, the spiritual idea of the divine Principle, Love, the true idea of God. Christ is also the divine manifestation of God, which comes to the flesh to destroy incarnate error, the ideal Truth that comes to heal sickness and sin.

Other teachings of Mrs. Eddy are that Christ is a spiritual divine emanation ; an impartation of God ; one with the infinite Mind. Man is an individualized expression of that Mind ; an individualization of the Christ ; governed by a perfect God, for ever perfect, imaging forth the infinite perfection of Mind, and with limitless powers.

The Christ Consciousness.

The last view of the Christ that I will now present is that the Christ consciousness is the capacity to know God. Each individual man consists of all the ideas that have ever come to him in the past, plus his capacity to know God, his power of being conscious of any idea he desires.

This capacity is the Christ capacity, and there is only one Christ capacity, which all men possess.

I was once thinking that I was wasting time when explaining Science to beginners, and I then recognized that if I treated whilst talking, I would be able to learn from them. A few days afterwards, recognizing this when speaking to my youngest son and treating, I had presented to me by him an idea which showed me that the Christ is the Christ capacity to know God, and, later on in the day, when asked, I treated and stated that in the 11th chapter of 1 Corinthians, Paul was not speaking of the material world at all, but of the spiritual world, and that when he said that "*the head of every man is Christ,*" he was referring to the fact that the Christ is the capacity which man has to know any idea of God that he needs, and that what may be spoken of as the actual doing of things is done by the consciousness, which consciousness appears in the material world as the body of a man.

Christ the True Idea of God and His Manifestation.

I found it rather difficult to unify the various views of the Christ, especially when Mrs. Eddy says that the Christ is the true idea of God, and also says that taking the illustration of the sun as God, the rays of light are the Christ, and each of us is a ray of light, until I found that these views are harmonized if one takes the Christ to be the true idea of God *and His manifestation.*

St. Paul's use of the word "*Christ,*" as meaning "all the spiritual beings in heaven," is not absolutely scientific, because it is really "the true idea of all the spiritual beings in heaven." Still, considering the difficulty there is in getting words to express spiritual facts, it is quite a legitimate use of the word.

"The Only Son of God" a Modern Concept.

The conception of Jesus as the only Son of God was of comparatively recent years. In the early creeds the word "*only*" (unicum) as applied to the Son of God is absent. It is not used in the creeds of Cyprian or Augustine; nor do Tertullian, Niceta, or even Novatian of Rome, use it. Valentinus taught in Rome between A.D. 140 and 160, the time when the Apostles' Creed is supposed to have been framed, and his school seems to have recognized the difference between Christ, the only begotten son, and Jesus the Christ, drawing attention to the fact that St. John wrote : "*We beheld his glory as of the only begotten*" (John 1 : 14), the word "*as*" differentiating the two.

Man is Divine.

The mistake that so many make is in relation to the teachings of Jesus the Christ that man is divine. Right throughout the Bible this is shown : "*God created man in his own image*" (Gen. 1 : 27). In Hosea 1 : 10, speaking of the present day, we read : "*It shall be said unto them, Ye are the sons of the living God.*" John says : "*Now are we the sons of God*" (1 John 3 : 2). Paul writes : "*Ye are the temple of the living God*" (2 Cor. 6 : 16). "*In him we live, and move, and have our being*" (Acts 17 : 28). "*The spirit of God hath made me*" (Job 33 : 4). "*For we are also his offspring*" (Aratus, quoted in Acts 17 : 28). Jesus put it stronger than any one else. He quoted the 82nd Psalm, and said, "*Ye are gods,*" and emphasized it by adding, "*and the scripture cannot be broken*" (John 10 : 34, 35). This he said to justify his statement, "*I am the Son of God.*" In Psalm 8 : 5, it is said that God made man "*a little lower than Elohim*" (Rev. Ver.) or God, and elsewhere in the Psalms and in many places the statement occurs that we are "*the sons of God.*" In the Authorized Version the word Elohim has been translated "*angels,*" for the translators, being so misled by matter, could not see that the real man is and always has been spiritual, and that, being made by God in His image and likeness, he never could fall, nor be material. Man conceives of God as man-like, instead of knowing man to be God-like.

We have to act up to this perfect ideal. Always mentally identify yourself with your real Self. "*We have a building of God, an house not made with hands, eternal in the heavens*" (2 Cor. 5 : 1). "*The kingdom of God is within you*" (Luke 17 : 21), within your present capacity of conscious realization. The marginal translation is still more accurate. "*The kingdom of God is among you*"—namely, heaven is not a future state to be reached by death. We make our own comparative heaven and our own hell by the way in which we think. Heaven is a perfect state of consciousness in which you always have been, you are now, and you always will be We are glorious children of a King, spiritual, eternal, and divine.

We see each other, however, falsely. As St. Paul says, " *We see through a glass, darkly* " (1 Cor. 13 : 12). Let the light of Truth in. See things as they really are. " *Now are we the sons of God* " (1 John 3 : 2) ; " *Ye are all the children of God* " (Gal. 3 : 26).   10

Few appear to grasp the far-reaching and glorious signification of Peter's reply to our Master, " *Thou art the Christ, the Son of the living God* " (Matt. 16 : 16).

Was Jesus Deity ?

It is comparatively easy to understand what the Christ is. The difficulty is as to the spiritual reality which was seen as the man Jesus. Three things our Lord might have been :

(1) The true idea of God seen materially.
(2) The true idea of the Logos, or Word.   20
(3) Or a spiritual being, part of God's infinite manifestation, one of the infinite number of beings in heaven, seen materially in a limited way.

In other words, was he Deity or was he only divine ? St. John evidently thought that he was the Logos or Word seen materially : " *And the Word was made flesh, and dwelt among us* " (John 1 : 14). I would like to prove that he was Deity, but intellectually I cannot see that he was. All that I can do is to keep a perfectly open mind, so as to be led by God to a knowledge of the 30 truth, realizing whenever I think of it that God is Truth and man knows Truth.

CHAPTER XVIII

THE HEALING OF SIN

A LTHOUGH there is not much difference between these various meanings of the Christ, still there is a distinction. The question is, How is one to prove what is the true meaning ? This can only be done by treatment. If you have sufficient knowledge, and can get a clear realization of the Christ, the person you are helping is healed instantaneously, whether it is of sin or disease.

10 One of my earliest cases of the healing of sin was when a man, who was a stranger to me, heard me talking to some people, and asked whether he might listen. Later he inquired whether he could come and see me at my office, as in those days I was in business. The next day he turned up and told me his sad story, and how sin had gripped him in its meshes.

He told me he was a married man with children, and that life to him was exactly like walking round and round the mouth of a burning volcano, knowing that sooner or 20 later he must tumble in. He was now so close to the end that it was as if his legs were being scorched the whole time, and yet he had no power to get away. His only escape seemed to be to take his life, but he did not like to do this for the sake of his wife and children, hoping that he might somehow find a means of gaining his freedom.

I explained to him that his sinning was not his fault, it was due to the condition of his so-called mind at his birth. Previously he was a victim ; now he had a means 30 of escape. This fact seemed to be a great relief to him, and he clearly saw that it was true. It is a great help to a sinner when you explain to him that he could not help sinning, that it was his misfortune and not his fault. He then gets back his self-respect, and when you show him the method of true prayer, whereby he can not only help himself but other sufferers out of their troubles, he goes on his way rejoicing.

Healed by the Realization of the Christ.

I explained to him that hitherto whenever I had been able to get a clear enough realization of the Christ, the person was healed, whether it was a case of sin or of disease ; I also told him that I had never had so bad a case of sin before, but that I would do my best. I then treated for him for about ten minutes, when I turned round and told him that I had got my realization as clear, I thought, as at any previous time, and that I did not think he would have any further trouble. 10

The last time I saw him, I think it was about six months after, he said that he had had no trouble of any kind. His medical man read a testimony at one of the testimony meetings which he had written out to be read. In this he said : " For many years I had a claim which is one of the worst forms of sin that man can possibly be attacked by. I had tried my hardest to get over it. Religion I tried for a long time, both Protestant and Roman Catholic, but it proved absolutely useless. My life at times was a hell, and I had terrible fits of de-20 pression. I seemed always over a volcano, with ruination of every kind staring me in the face, and no way of escape." At the end of the testimony he wrote : " I felt that I was cured, and this turned out to be the case ; I also felt another man, and that I had been born again, and am now free, and happiness has come to me. I hope now that I shall be able to prove my gratitude by my life. I have already found that I am able to get instantaneous results by turning out the wrong thoughts, and realizing the perfect man in the way I have been shown, and I 30 believe that I shall be the means of dragging many of my fellow-victims out of the slough of despond into which they have fallen." Once we know how to pray rightly we understand the following words of our Lord : " *Come unto me, all ye that labour and are heavy laden, and I will give you rest. Take my yoke upon you, and learn of me . . . for my yoke is easy, and my burden is light* " (Matt. 11 : 28–30).

The Healing of Sin the Only Proof.

The healing of sin is the only absolute proof of the 40 truth of the teachings herein set out. All the other wonderful results mentioned can be obtained with the

human mind if a person is hypnotic enough. The reason for this is that all matter is merely mental phenomena, and by strong thinking you can cause matter to appear or disappear. You cannot, however, permanently heal a man of sin, because to do this, looking at it from a natural science point of view, you have to purify the cell in the subconscious mind by the short-circuiting of the particles that damp down the cell, so that it no longer vibrates with the evil thoughts when they attack. This destruc-
10 tion of the particles can only be done, speaking from a theological point of view, by the action of God. It is true that by hypnotism and mental suggestion you can temporarily relieve a man from such a thing as a tendency to drink, but trouble always arises. A friend of mine, a medical man, was at one time one of the three leading authorities in England on hypnotism. He told me that he could keep a man from drink by regularly hypnotizing him every three months. Once he had as a patient a man who was addicted to drink, and by hypnotizing him
20 every three months he kept him free. One year he went away for his holiday, and, whilst away, forgot altogether that the time had arrived for the patient to be hypnotized. The result was that the man had a bout of drinking and cut his throat. This, he said, made him give up trying to protect people in this way. This friend of mine had great experience, and was a man who tried to do his very best for humanity, and the case is a very representative one of the evils attached to hypnotic work. People must not imagine that wonderful results cannot be obtained ;
30 they can, but they are not obtained from the destruction of matter, as when one turns in thought to God, but by altering the electric tension which, as I have pointed out, merely leads to some other form of trouble attacking the subject.

As compared with this I may give my own experience with regard to the healing of sin. For over eighteen years after I started, I never had a man come to me for the healing of sin where the result was not instantaneous, and only in one case was there any return. This was a
40 case of drink that I have already mentioned, where I had to give the man two further treatments. The case of failure was that of a man in the army who wrote asking for help, but he did not tell me what was the trouble.

Two or three days afterwards he was shot. As far as I
could tell it seemed that the difficulty was due to other
people who were forcing him into the sin. In a case of
this sort in order to get temporary relief it is best to give
the major portion of the time available to treating, so
to speak, for the other people, *i.e.* to destroy the evil
thoughts that act upon the others and make them think
strongly that the man will join with them in the sin.
Then the thoughts causing the trouble are destroyed,
instead of the evil vibrations being increased, and you get 10
the time to change the mind of the patient permanently,
so that no wrong thoughts will again harm him.

Results the Only Proof of Anything.

In the cases of instantaneous healing of sin, I feel
sure that in some the mind was immediately completely
changed and purified, so far as the particular sin went,
because I only gave one treatment. In other cases, the
evil thoughts tempting the patient were destroyed by the
denial, and I had to go on treating every day until the
mind was changed. When I first started and had com- 20
paratively only a few patients, after the person was
apparently healed and was no longer ostensibly a patient,
I used to continue to treat regularly every day for him,
so as to make certain of the permanent change of his
mind. In some cases I went on from three to six months.
I think it is probably due to this that in the early cases,
as with the later ones, as far as I am aware, there has
never been any return of any serious trouble like consumption, cancer, fibroid tumour, goitre, etc., even where
there was only one direct treatment given. I think this 30
instantaneous healing of sin and permanent healing of
disease is not so much due to the fact that one was always
treating in the highest way, *i.e.* by the realization of
God, but that the action of God has prevented cases coming to me that were beyond my ability to heal permanently. The results are an absolutely conclusive proof to
those who work in a different way, that the method in
which one works, *i.e.* solely by the realization of God, is
correct. There is no proof of any theory but results.

We all agree with the words of St. Paul : " *For what* 40
I would, that do I not ; but what I hate, that do I "
(Rom. 7 : 15). The only way in which we can alter this

is by true prayer, by the realization of God and God's perfect world. This leads to freedom from sin, disease, and fear. Our Lord put it more strongly than anyone else; he said: "*Be ye therefore perfect, even as your Father which is in heaven is perfect*" (Matt. 5 : 48). The only method of reaching this ideal state is shown by the Prophet Isaiah as follows : "*Look unto me, and be ye saved, all the ends of the earth: for I am God, and there is none else*" (Isa. 45 : 22). The result of working in this way is that "*they shall teach no more every man his neighbour, and every man his brother, saying, Know the Lord: for they shall all know me, from the least of them unto the greatest of them, saith the Lord: for I will forgive their iniquity, and I will remember their sin no more*" (Jer. 31 : 34). "*And it shall be said in that day, Lo, this is our God; we have waited for him, and he will save us*" (Isa. 25 : 9).

In the Wisdom of Solomon we read : "*The ungodly said . . . Let us oppress the poor righteous man. . . . He professeth to have the knowledge of God: and he calleth himself the child of the Lord. . . . We are esteemed of him as counterfeits: . . . he pronounceth the end of the just to be blessed, and maketh his boast that God is his father. Let us see if his words be true*" (ch. 2 : 1, 10, 13, 16, 17).

Fortunately you need not believe a word of what is herein stated. In fact, you ought not to believe it. If you do, you are building upon the beliefs of an individual who may be right or may be wrong. Make certain that you understand the meaning of what is written, and then test it and prove it for yourself. "*Prove me now herewith, said the Lord of hosts, if I will not open you the windows of heaven, and pour you out a blessing, that there shall not be room enough to receive it*" (Mal. 3 : 10).

Right away from the start you can get results. They may at first be small, but they prove the principle, and there is no proof of any theory, except results. "*These signs shall follow them that believe; In my name shall they cast out devils; they shall speak with new tongues; they shall take up serpents; and if they drink any deadly thing, it shall not hurt them; they shall lay hands on the sick, and they shall recover*" (Mark 16 : 17, 18).

The so-called miracles were not limited to the apostles.

Our Lord said : " *He that believeth on me* (the " true nature of man," translated " name " in the Bible), *the works that I do shall he do also ; and greater works than these shall he do* " (John 14 : 12). In fact, no theory is of the slightest value except for the benefits which can be obtained from putting it into practice.

" Prove all Things."

Finally, do not give up anything you believe that makes you and those around you better and happier, until you find something still better, something which will help you to be purer in thought, more loving, more thoughtful for others—in fact, a better man. In the words of St. Paul : " *Prove all things ; hold fast that which is good* " (1 Thess. 5 : 21). You will then build up your knowledge upon ascertained facts and not upon what other people think, and will gain the knowledge of " *the peace of God which passeth all understanding* " (Phil. 4 : 7).

"WATCH AND PRAY"

WE have to watch our thoughts continually. *"Watch and pray"* and *"Pray without ceasing."* This means that directly we think a wrong thought, that is, even any thought that is not harmonious, we have to drive it out of our mind, and cease thinking of things material, raising the level of our thoughts until we are thinking only of God, and things spiritual, *i.e.* truly mental.

10 One method of doing this is to split up our thoughts into three heads :

First.—**Turn in thought to God and heaven.** This is absolutely essential. It does not matter much what your concept is, provided it is your best idea of the glorious world called heaven.

Second.—**Deny the existence in heaven of the wrong thing thought of, seen, or felt.** When, for instance, you see an angry man, or feel angry, realize, whilst thinking of heaven, that there is no such thing as anger in that 20 spiritual kingdom, the kingdom of heaven, the reality.

This is called the denial or Angel Michael.

Third.—**Realize the existence of the opposite**—namely, in the case of anger, whilst still thinking of heaven, realize that in that perfect world, the world of reality, all is peace and love. Think of God as Love, and the spiritual man as absolutely loving. Dwell on this realization and get it as clear as possible.

This is called the affirmation or Angel Gabriel.

If there is then time, it is advisable to split up one's 30 thoughts into two more heads, namely :

Fourth.—**Realize why this is so**—namely, because God, the Principle of good, rules and governs all ; because there is nothing but God and His manifestation in the spiritual kingdom, the world of reality, called heaven.

Fifth.—**Try to form as clear an idea as you can of God** and His manifestation, heaven.

Reversing our thoughts in this way all day long is prayer without ceasing, and is leading us continually to abide " *in the secret place of the most High* " (Ps. 91 : 1). It also teaches us clearly and perpetually to recognize that all sin, disease, worry, limitations, etc.—being merely the effect of wrong thinking—are non-realities, *i.e.* have no permanence about them. It causes us also to realize the truth, namely, that God and His manifestation are spiritual and perfect, All-in-all, omni-present.

Do not take this as a hard-and-fast rule of working. 10 Let God teach you the way to work, not man.

INDEX